EVERLASTING
HOPE

Inspirational messages that encourage,

motivate, and heal in any situation

CHARISMA
HOUSE

Most Charisma House Book Group products are available at special quantity discounts for bulk purchase for sales promotions, premiums, fund-raising, and educational needs. For details, write Charisma House Book Group, 600 Rinehart Road, Lake Mary, Florida 32746, or telephone (407) 333-0600.

Everlasting Hope edited by Charisma House
Published by Charisma House
Charisma Media/Charisma House Book Group
600 Rinehart Road
Lake Mary, Florida 32746
www.charismahouse.com

Cover design by Lisa Rae Cox
Design Director: Bill Johnson

Library of Congress Cataloging-in-Publication Data:
An application to register this book for cataloging has been submitted to the Library of Congress.
International Standard Book Number: 978-1-62136-617-1
E-book ISBN: 978-1-62136-618-8

First edition

14 15 16 17 18 — 9 8 7 6 5 4 3 2 1
Printed in the United States of America

CONTENTS

BECAUSE YOU HOPE IN HIM

*...and hope does not disappoint, because the love
of God has been poured out within our hearts
through the Holy Spirit who was given to us.*

—ROMANS 5:5, NAS

ACCORDING TO WEBSTER's dictionary, the word *hope* is
a verb, meaning "to cherish a desire with anticipation,"
"to desire with expectation of obtainment," and "to expect
with confidence." Hope is an action word that is all about
expectation. When you hope for something, you have an
expectation that it will be delivered to you. You are confident that whatever it is, it is coming your way.

But how many times have you been let down when
you've hoped against hope and were so sure that what you
were promised, imagining, or worked for was coming your
way? How many times have you not gotten what you hoped
for? How many times have you gotten your hopes up, only
to be disappointed?

These days it's hard to have confident expectation for
anything. One day the stock market is up; the next day it's
down. One day you're the go-to person at work; the next

you're in the unemployment line. One day your marriage is blissful; the next day you're faced with major conflict.

Placing your hope in things, opportunities, and people and being disappointed and let down over and over again can make your heart sick. The Bible calls this "hope deferred" (Prov. 13:12). What you have been expecting has been delayed—indefinitely. This is what leads to hopelessness, discouragement, and sometimes even depression, stress, and anxiety. We know these emotions are bad on our hearts both physically and spiritually.

What if there was a way for you to build up your hope and never be disappointed? What if there was a way for you to always know that what is promised will come through? I challenge you to believe that this is indeed possible. When your hope is built on nothing less than Jesus's blood and His righteousness, you will never be let down, overlooked, or forgotten. Jesus will not pass you by. He has made a way for you. All that you hope for and desire is in Him.

Proverbs 13:12 says that when the desire we have comes, it is a tree of life. In other words you are fulfilled, fruitful, prosperous, and full of vitality. What if you reframed your perception of desire and realized that when it all comes down to it, Jesus is your one true desire. He is all you need. Every hope you have can be placed in Him, and you will never suffer from a sickened heart.

We are all guilty of hoping in jobs, opportunities, or approval from people, but let me say that all of these desires have the potential to fail. Jesus never fails.

In this book I have compiled some of the most encouraging and challenging messages on hope from Charisma House's best-selling authors. This book is custom made just for you to help you replant your hopes in good, 100 percent guaranteed, Jesus Christ ground.

Let's start by declaring our hope in God, right now.

I declare that the eye of the Lord is on me because I fear Him and hope in His mercy (Ps. 33:18).

I declare that the Lord will let His mercy be upon me, because I hope in Him (Ps. 33:22).

I am full of courage because I hope in the Lord (Ps. 31:24).

I will wait for the Lord, and in His word I do hope (Ps. 130:5).

I declare that I am blessed because I trust in the Lord and my hope is in Him (Jer. 17:7).

I declare that I am happy because the God of Jacob is my help. My hope is in Him (Ps. 146:5).

I declare that the Lord takes pleasure in me, because I hope in His mercy (Ps. 147:11).

My hope will not be cut off (Prov. 23:18).

I rejoice in hope, am patient in tribulation, and continue steadfastly in prayer (Rom. 12:12).

I declare that I am filled with the love of God, therefore, I will not lose hope, for love hopes all things (1 Cor. 13:7).

I declare that Jesus, my one desire, comes to me. He is my tree of life (Prov. 13:12).

I declare that my hope will not be disappointed, because I hope in Christ, my Savior (Rom. 5:5).

I pray that this book, *Everlasting Hope*, blesses you. I pray that you are set on a high place after reading this book. I pray that your hopes will be firmly planted on the rock of Jesus Christ. I pray that your spiritual muscles will be strengthened so that when you are tempted to put your hope in any earthly thing over God, you will resist and continue to hope in the faithful One. I pray that you will hold on to your hope and never give up, because God won't give up on you!

Peace, hope, love, and blessing on you all your days,

—JEVON BOLDEN
IMPRINT EDITOR, CHARISMA HOUSE

PART 1

HOPE THROUGH DISAPPOINTMENT, REJECTION, AND FAILURE

Chapter 1

MOVING FROM
DISAPPOINTMENT TO DESTINY

*Then Hannah prayed and said: "My heart rejoices in
the LORD; in the LORD my horn is lifted high. . . . She
who was barren has borne seven children. . . . He raises
the poor from the dust and lifts the needy from the ash
heap; he seats them with princes and has them inherit a
throne of honor. . . . He will guard the feet of his saints."*

—1 SAMUEL 2:1–9, NIV

HAVE YOU EVER had a dream dissolve? Have you ever
longed for something, prayed for it, put your heart,
soul, mind, and body into it, only to fail to see it come to
pass? You had everything in order, and you just knew God
wanted this to happen—yet it didn't.[*]

Why does God allow disappointment in our lives? If He
is a good Father who desires to give good gifts to His children, why does He allow our dreams to be tested?

---

* Terry Crist, *Awakened to Destiny* (Lake Mary, FL: Charisma House,
2002), 167, 177–180, 183–185, 187.

There are times when God allows everything to quiet down in our lives. He brings us into momentary seasons of holdback, momentary times of confinement—not because of judgment or because He is angry with us, but simply because He wants to bring our character up to the measure of our dreams. God wants us to know that He values us because of who we are, not because of what we do.

Sometimes we need to remind ourselves that our worth in the eyes of the Father and the favor He bestows on us are not based upon how well we perform. He loves us if we cycle from failure to failure, and disappointment to disappointment. It's not our responsibility to uphold God's reputation throughout all of the earth. Thank God, it is not my responsibility to be the model of a perfect leader or a perfect pastor. It is my responsibility to be God's son, to delight in my sonship, to take my identity from His fatherhood, and to be obedient to His passion for my life. If I do that, everything in my life is successful no matter what it looks like to others. God is more interested in what we become than in what we accomplish.

Disappointment simply means, "Not as planned or appointed." One of our greatest struggles in life is with issues that do not go as we planned. When our hopes and dreams fail to materialize within the time frame we have allotted for them, we grow faint of heart.

Disappointment in Our Circumstances

Circumstances can bring great disappointment. There are times when we can't find anyone or anything to blame—except the pain of being human. We know that God is good. We know that the people around us did everything right. We know that it wasn't any failure of our own. It was simply the circumstances. We live in a sin-ravaged, sin-cursed world. Daily we fight an enemy who wants to destroy us, ruin our marriages, abort our prosperity, or paralyze our ministry. We were born in war. We live in war. We will die in war. Until Jesus comes back and ends the war, we are consigned to life on a battlefield—and casualties often occur. People get sick. Some die. Some go bankrupt. Some lose ministries. Life leads us through many transitional processes, but through it all we can be confident in the fact that we are sons and daughters of the Most High God.

There is a remarkable story found in 1 Samuel, chapters 1 and 2. It is the story of a woman who went from having a dream through great disappointment and, ultimately, to her destiny. Her name was Hannah.

Hannah's dream was to have a child. In particular, she wanted a son. This was complicated by the fact her husband had two wives. In this environment, rife with competition, jealously, strife, and hurt, we hear the pathos in these words, "Hannah had no children" (1 Sam. 1:2, NKJV). Barrenness in ancient times was the ultimate tragedy for a married woman. Every man wanted a male heir to perpetuate his name and to inherit his estate. Barrenness was also considered a sign of divine punishment—of spiritual rejection. And yet year after year Hannah struggled with an unfulfilled dream, a misunderstanding husband, a heartless rival, and devastating disappointment.

Here was a woman torn by two conflicts—at times she felt that God was punishing her for something of which she was unaware; other times she felt that her husband was disappointed in her for not providing the son for which she—and he—desperately longed. In spite of her husband's reassurance and love, Hannah felt less than a whole woman because of her barrenness. But Hannah had a dream. She believed for a son. And in spite of her misery, shame, ridicule, rejection, and embarrassment, the power of that dream worked in her life, and that dream sustained her.

Hannah sets a wonderful example for us. First, she is brutally honest about her true feelings. She doesn't try to put on a spiritual show for anyone and say, "Well, praise God, it doesn't matter if I have children or not. I'm just fine." She admitted that she was deeply troubled, bitter, and in great anguish and grief. But Hannah also prayed. In her disappointment and grief she did not turn away from God.

Hannah's story reminds us of God's unswerving faithfulness. In the course of time Hannah conceived and gave birth to a son. When her dream became a reality, she didn't forget God. Hannah kept her promise, and she dedicated the child, Samuel, to the Lord. She weaned him at the age of three, as Hebrew mothers did, and took him to the temple. Then God blessed her with five more children.

By trusting God and staying faithful during times of temptation, testing, and trial, Hannah moved from a dream through disappointment and into her destiny, and so can you. But you have to be willing to persevere. Overcoming the challenges of life is not as easy as following a twelve-step process for success—it is about releasing the need to succeed. When nothing else will satisfy you but the fulfillment of your dreams, you have begun the journey toward your destiny.

Chapter 2

THE STORY OF BARSABBAS

God causes all things to work together for
good to those who love God, to those who
are called according to His purpose.

—ROMANS 8:28, NAS

IT HAD ALL the trappings of a final interview. The breath mints. The posture. The etiquette. The maneuvering to make that good first impression. The arriving thirty minutes early with the look of "this is part of my normal work ethic." There were the competitive but friendly smiles exchanged between applicants as they crossed paths in the lobby. The finalists were both ready and sweaty.*

The pay package? Retirement? Well, maybe these weren't the pressing issues with this particular job. But still, both men had high hopes that the job was theirs. The job posting did have one oddity that needs mentioning. The last man to hold this job committed suicide. That alone should have

---

* Scott Hagan, *They Felt the Spirit's Touch* (Lake Mary, FL: Charisma House, 2003), 35–41.

been a warning to these final two candidates as to what the "office" job was all about. But the two stood willing. They were Matthias and Barsabbas.

The disciples looked around the room. The Eleven quickly caucused. Some among the Eleven thought it was Matthias. Others thought Barsabbas was the choice.

They decided to let God have the final vote.

The decision for the next apostle wasn't going to come down to who had the right breath, the right clothes, and the right moxie in front of the right people. The selection process hinged upon a simple word revealed in the apostles' prayer. "And they prayed and said, 'You, Lord, who know the hearts of all men, show which one of these two You have chosen to occupy this ministry and apostleship from which Judas turned aside to go to his own place'" (Acts 1:24–25, NAS).

God's criteria went where no man could look: H-E-A-R-T.

The process of "lots" was simple. Two names were written on either two stones or two separate pieces of parchment and placed in an urn. Someone trustworthy from the congregation was then chosen to come forward and draw one of the names out of the "hat." This allowed God to direct the choice. With the Upper Room silent, a stone was selected. On it, the name Matthias was written.

As godly as Matthias was, he was still human. And humans get excited when they are chosen over someone else to do important stuff. Be it student council or team captain, we love to be chosen. We also hate being rejected.

No doubt Barsabbas, the unchosen stone, hugged Matthias and congratulated him on his selection. No doubt he remained spiritual, humble, and positive. At least on the outside.

There are some days when the lot lets you down. Just ask Barsabbas. He had just finished second in a race of two. Being a silver medalist suddenly didn't feel like such an accomplishment.

It was character that got you this far, Barsabbas, but sorry, God has picked someone else.

It was time for Matthias to move on with the Twelve. It was time for Barsabbas to go quietly back to his seat. And poor Barsabbas, not only did he not get the job, but to this day he also suffers from name confusion. Ask ten Christians who Barsabbas was, and seven of them will tell you he was the guy Pilate let go from prison in favor of Jesus. The other three think he traveled as a missionary with Paul.

Barsabbas was learning a tough lesson. Maybe God chose him to go through it for the rest of us. As much as I would like to think that is possible, I know differently. All of us go through this moment, but as least we know we're not alone.

Maybe the real chosen one was Barsabbas, not Matthias. Maybe the assignment of modeling joy through disappointment and rejection is what God was after all along. Here are three things Barsabbas could take away from this experience.

1. The best things that happen in life are sometimes the things that do not happen.

2. The will of God is sometimes the wall of God.

3. We tend to learn far more from the word *no* than we do from the word *yes*.

Our hearts are tested by disappointment. What good purpose could this experience have served Barsabbas's life? Why bait him and then burst his bubble? Why not just have one candidate? Why take the risk of a hurt? Yes, the story teaches us that God can see where man cannot. And yes, it teaches that there are standards and qualifications for those who lead us.

But it teaches even louder through Barsabbas that we must triumph over times of personal disappointment. Over those times when we are certain God has opened a door, then after sharing our plans, the door never opens. We feel as if we have egg on our faces. We are left embarrassed...sometimes even disillusioned with God. Romans 8:28 tells us, "God causes all things to work together for good to those who love God, to those who are called according to His purpose" (NAS).

But the Word of God promises that when we "love God," He will cause "all things to work together for good." Loving God is the equivalent to inviting a master artist to approach your canvas with permission to paint as he sees fit. As Jesus paints the canvas with beauty, substance, and purpose, a great miracle begins to unfold. In His mercy Jesus chooses to integrate our past into the current and future picture of our lives. Sometimes it takes time for the work of the Artist to make sense. You wonder why He forgives the sin but leaves the stones. Why?

Because He promised to use "all things." In other words,

He takes our painful history and, through grace, incorporates it into our portrait.

When the Artist is given enough time, He will turn your life into a work of art for the world to see. He will use "all things together" for His good. The painful things. The broken things. The rejected things. But the key is love. Not just God's love toward you, but also your love toward Him.

Barsabbas will probably tell me in heaven that I made way too much out of this. That he was fine with not being chosen as Judas Iscariot's replacement. I guess I will have to believe him. But for now, he's one of my secret heroes of Acts.

And by the way, Barsabbas didn't totally disappear. He showed up one more time in Acts 15. They needed a delegation of highly loving and sensitive individuals who could tenderly hand-deliver an important document on behalf of the early church leadership. They chose Barsabbas (Acts 15:22).

Oh, by the way, the retirement package Matthias got for his "office" job was a killer. He was stoned by the Jews.

Chapter 3

LIFE'S DESERT PLACES

*Therefore I am now going to allure her; I will lead
her into the desert and speak tenderly to her.*

—Hosea 2:14, niv

THE PEOPLE OF Israel went hungry in the desert after
leaving Egypt. They grumbled against Moses and
Aaron as they remembered the bread they ate in Egypt
until they were filled (Exod. 16:1–3). God gave them manna,
telling them, "In the morning you will see the glory of the
Lord" (v. 7, niv).*

In John's Gospel Jesus makes Himself known as "the
true bread from heaven" (John 6:32–35, niv). He identified
His own body with the figure of the manna.

A desert is a desolate place where the most basic elements
for survival are lacking. God tries our faith in the desert.
"He humbled you, causing you to hunger and then feeding
you with manna, which neither you nor your fathers had

---

* Claudio Freidzon, *Holy Spirit, I Hunger for You* (Lake Mary, FL: Charisma House, 1997), 17–18, 21–27.

known, to teach you that man does not live on bread alone but on every word that comes from the mouth of the LORD" (Deut. 8:3, NIV). In this way He causes us to cry out before Him, acknowledging His supernatural, daily provision.

Again and again God has proven His faithfulness in the midst of my terrible deserts. At times when I was unable to provide a meal for my family, God, in His mercy, provided for us even though I sometimes complained, as the people of Israel did. Many times my father-in-law, who owned a grocer's shop, turned up when our closet was empty. The popular saying that God pays on the date of expiration has a lot of truth in it. He wants us to grow in faith!

I want to share with you an even deeper lesson from this passage. Sometimes we will be asked to choose between material bread and the spiritual bread that comes from the mouth of the Lord.

In the middle of a desert what would your priorities be? If we choose to work eagerly to solve our problems, running here and there before we turn our faces toward God, we will be putting the cart before the horse.

A desert offers a wonderful opportunity to meet with God and hear His words to us. God is there, calling attention to Himself. "Therefore I am now going to allure her; I will lead her into the desert and speak tenderly to her" (Hosea 2:14, NIV). God makes us feel hungry in order to feed us with His Holy Spirit, and then He showers favor and mercy on us.

Are you being tried? Fast, pray, and groan before God. Seek the real bread that comes down from heaven! This is your deepest need.

When Jesus withdrew to fast and pray in the desert, the

devil appeared in order to tempt Him. (See Matthew 4:1–11.) It was a moment of need for Jesus, and the devil tried to sway His attention from things above to earthly things by challenging Him to turn stones into bread. Jesus rebuked him by quoting this text: "It is written: 'Man does not live on bread alone, but on every word that comes from the mouth of God'" (Matt. 4:4, NIV). In your desert the devil will offer you hundreds of solutions and alternatives except one: to seek earnestly the face of God.

This is a lesson I learned through the many deserts God brought me through. My deserts are part of the roots of my walk with Christ. I could never disown them. Because I walked through them, I can understand you and encourage you with all of my heart. Move forward! God has a marvelous plan for your life, and when the time comes, you will know what it is. Your present moment is of great value to God. He is preparing you, equipping you, to use you powerfully. Only remember one thing, the most important thing: seek Him.

Chapter 4

GOING ON WHEN YOUR
WANT TO IS GONE

*Looking unto Jesus, the author and finisher of
our faith, who for the joy that was set before Him
endured the cross, despising the shame, and has sat
down at the right hand of the throne of God.*

—HEBREWS 12:2, NKJV

HANGING ON A CROSS isn't an experience that evokes
thoughts of joy.* Dying on a cross was one of the
most cruel and painful ways a person could die. Yet while
hanging on the cross, Jesus prayed for His accusers, "Father,
forgive them; for they know not what they do" (Luke 23:34,
KJV). He didn't feel sorry for Himself, and He wasn't angry.
Why? Because Jesus focused on the joy He would experience and share with His father and His followers when He
finally defeated death and the grave.

America's slogan is becoming, "If at first you don't

---

* Mike Purkey, *Reversing the Devil's Decision* (Lake Mary, FL: Charisma
House, 2000), 104–107.

succeed, lower your standards." For some of us, our slogan is, "If at first you don't succeed, do it the way your wife told you to do it the first time." But to succeed in life you have to have endurance.

We need to learn how to pull ourselves up by our bootstraps and develop a Holy Spirit toughness. Jesus said, "I have given you authority to trample on snakes and scorpions and to overcome all the power of the enemy; nothing will harm you" (Luke 10:19, NIV). We have the power of God resident within us to overturn every decision the devil has made for us, including his decision to make us give up.

Let's take off our nice, religious masks and be honest. We all face times in our lives when we would like to give up. There are times when quitting church looks good. There are times when giving up our jobs looks good.

There comes a time in every marriage when quitting looks good. There are even times when giving up on God looks good. The grass is always greener on the other side of the fence. So we think, "If I was over *there* instead of over *here*, I would be happier." But if you think you have problems now, jump to the other side of the fence!

The Reason to Keep Going

When you keep getting up into adversity's face, adversity finally has to say, "Oh, no! He's back up again. He's got the Word of God in his hand. He has a testimony in his mouth. He has praise in his heart, and he's coming back! Every time I think I'm about to overtake him, he gets back up again!"

Can you ever be sure when you give up that you weren't

right at the doorway to your answer? There are some who quit God just days before their miracle was going to be manifested in their lives. That's like some people who go through college for four years and then drop out two or three months before graduation. That's not very smart. But it's not nearly as unintelligent as people who have hung in there, prayed, and stood their ground and then all of a sudden quit just about the time that their new job was about to materialize or their children were going to come back to the Lord. You can't give up!

Satan is terrified of God's children when they're determined to keep swimming despite the fog and frigid waters. He's terrified of a Simon Peter who is willing to get out of the boat and walk on the waters of faith. Satan's not afraid of someone sitting pitifully in a pool of despair saying, "I'm in this mess because of somebody else."

You have to take the Word of God and put it right under the devil's throat and let him know, "I'll be here tomorrow, same time, same station, so just get used to seeing my face and get used to this sword sticking in your gut!"

If you were the devil and you kept getting run through with the sword of the Spirit every time you picked on a person, wouldn't you get tired of it? That first thrust may not bother you, but after the third or fourth time it could get irritating. By the fifth or sixth time getting skewered in the same place could get downright painful. Whatever decision the devil has made regarding your life, strike back with the name of Jesus and what the Word says about that decision.

Chapter 5

GOD'S AMAZING GRACE WILL
COVER YOUR FAILURES

*But where sin abounded, grace abounded much
more, so that as sin reigned in death, even so
grace might reign through righteousness to
eternal life through Jesus Christ our Lord.*

—ROMANS 5:20–21, NKJV

IN HABAKKUK 1:5 God told the people of Jerusalem that
He would do some amazing things through them.* Read
aloud what the Word of God says:

Look at the nations and watch—and be utterly
amazed. For I am going to do something in your
days that you would not believe, even if you were
told.

—NIV

---

* Babbie Mason, *Faith Lift* (Lake Mary, FL: Charisma House, 2003),
93–96.

As I read the Bible, I have gotten in the practice of putting my name in the place of the nouns and pronouns as they refer to the people of God. Then I claim that promise as if it were written to me personally. You should try that. It will give you a boost, a faith-filled mind-set. The Bible was written to you and me personally. Every promise in the Book, from cover to cover, belongs to us personally.

When it comes to God turning messes into blessings, the story of a great hymn writer comes to mind. John Newton, a white Englishman, left home and school at the age of eleven to begin life as a rough, depraved seaman. Eventually he became involved in the despicably evil occupation of buying and selling slaves, capturing them from their native land of West Africa and selling them around the world. As a slave trader, he preyed on the lives of black Africans, mercilessly tearing them away from their families and separating them from their homeland. This wicked man was even known to have victimized countless women slaves while aboard a slave ship.

Years later, while at sea, John Newton was caught in a fierce storm. Stunned with fear and afraid of shipwreck, he cried out to God for help. God rescued him. This incident led him to a dramatic conversion experience that would change John Newton's life forever. God saved this man, cleansed him of a dreadful past, restored him to his rightful mind and gave him a clean heart and a brand-new start. Soon he began sensing that God was calling him to study for the ministry. This man, who once called himself a "wretch," became an ordained minister of the Anglican Church in a little village of Olney, England. Greatly influenced by John and Charles Wesley, his friends and fellow colleagues in the ministry and fellow songwriters, Newton began to use simple hymns in his service rather than just using the Psalms.

Wanting to express his own testimony in the form of a song, one morning John Newton introduced from the pulpit of his church a new song that God had blessed him to compose. He wanted this song to tell what God had done for him. That song was the great hymn "Amazing Grace."

> Amazing grace! How sweet the sound,
> That saved a wretch like me!
> I once was lost, but now am found,
> Was blind, but now I see.[1]

The unique thing about this hymn is that the melody is written on the pentatonic scale. The tune is centered around the five black notes on the keyboard of the piano. The Negro spirituals that were brought to America by African slaves were written and sung on the pentatonic or five-note scale. "Amazing Grace," whose powerful lyrics were written by a white man from England, is an African melody line.

Isn't that just like God to use a melody that John Newton certainly heard coming from the belly of his own slave ship? Isn't it like God to use a life marred by sin to birth something so simple, yet so profound? This melody was moaned by African men and women, homesick for a land they would never see again and terrified of what lay ahead. As those melodies, songs of grief and angst, swelled up out of the slave hold below, the Holy Spirit lay hold of John Newton's heart and planted a seed that would reap a song that would be sung around the world. Only God could use a life that was once filled with disgrace, and one who thought nothing of disgracing others, to birth one of the most beautiful hymns that the world has ever sung.

> 'Twas grace that taught my heart to fear,
> And grace my fears relieved;
> How precious did that grace appear
> The hour I first believed.[2]

The apostle Paul tells us, "Where sin abounded, grace did much more abound" (Rom. 5:20, KJV). Grace. No matter how deep into sin you may have fallen, grace will go deeper still. If God can change a man whose lustful heart was filled with hatred and wrath, a man the likes of John Newton, surely God is able to change your heart and shout a proclamation of grace at the obstacles in your life and bring them crashing down. Maybe you have disgraced yourself and others by committing some unforgiveable act. Did you make a mistake by prejudging someone before you knew all the facts? Have you condemned yourself or someone else, and your heart is cluttered with anger and resentment, even hatred?

You may have a reputation that has preceded you, and what others think and say about you is true. But God is able to do an "about faith" in your life to turn things around for you. God is able to replace your disgrace, anger, resentment, bitterness, disappointment, disillusionment, disgust, and even hatred with joy unspeakable and full of glory. Give all the messes you have created with your life to Jesus. He can handle it. He wants you to know today that there is nothing you could ever do that could keep Him from loving you. Romans 8:38–39 fills my heart with boundless hope and raises my faith to a new level:

> For I am persuaded, that neither death, nor life, nor angels, nor principalities, nor powers, nor things present, nor things to come, nor height, nor depth, nor any other creature, shall be able to separate us from the love of God, which is in Christ Jesus our Lord.
>
> —KJV

I believe that covers everything. Do you believe it too?

PART 2

HOPE THROUGH FEAR

Chapter 6

THE SPIRIT OF INTIMIDATION

For God did not give us a spirit of timidity, but a
spirit of power, of love and of self-discipline.
—2 TIMOTHY 1:7, NIV

IN ORDER TO recognize and deal with intimidation—or
fear—we must be settled on two issues. First, fear, or
timidity, is a spirit, and second, it is not from God. "For
God did not give us a spirit of timidity" (2 Tim. 1:7, NIV).*

The Greek word for *spirit* in this passage is *pneuma*,
which is the same word used for the Holy Spirit or the
spirit of man or a demon, according to Strong's concor-
dance. Intimidation is not an attitude or a disposition. It
is a *spirit*.

Since intimidation is a spirit, it cannot be fought on the
level of our intellect or will. Having a positive mental attitude will not overcome intimidation. Spiritual resistance

---

* John Bevere, *Breaking Intimidation* (Lake Mary, FL: Charisma House,
1995, 2006), 48–49, 69–70, 83–84, 90, 154.

requires spiritual assistance. It must be addressed in the realm of the spirit.

Consider this: Why would people who are intelligent and physically strong struggle with intimidation—often from someone or something weaker in body and mind? Perhaps everything is fine, but they live in constant dread that their circumstances might change for the worse. They spend all their time and energy worrying and trying to safeguard themselves against what may never happen. It is impossible for them to enjoy the present because they are so afraid of their future. It doesn't make sense, yet no matter how you reason with them, their fear persists. They have a spirit of timidity, or fear. They are not fighting natural weakness but spiritual weakness.

Symptoms of Intimidation

An intimidating spirit unleashes confusion, discouragement, and frustration. Its goal is to cause you to lose your proper perspective. Everything will seem overwhelming, difficult, or even impossible. The stronger the intimidation, the greater the discouragement and hopelessness. If intimidation is not dealt with immediately, it will cause you to do things you would never do if you were not under its influence.

The goal of intimidation is to make us give up our authority, thereby rendering our gifts inoperative. We are then reduced to operating in our own limited strength and ability. This usually changes our position from offensive to defensive. Then, aware that we are vulnerable, we further retreat to what is comfortable and safe.

Examining instances when I've been attacked by an intimidating spirit, I can relate to what Elijah must have felt when he came up against Jezebel. Before I understood how intimidation worked, I would sit in my hotel room fighting discouragement and hopelessness. I would wonder, "What good is all this doing? Who do you think you are?" I would sometimes have thoughts in the morning after a great service.

I recall one particular time when I could do absolutely nothing all day. I couldn't shake the heaviness. I would pray, and it seemed God was nowhere. Just as with Elijah, my focus had shifted to me, me, me. I felt ineffective; I considered my ministry to be worthless. That is why Elijah said, "It is enough! Now, LORD, take my life, for I am no better than my fathers!" (1 Kings 19:4, NKJV).

At the end of this particularly discouraging day, God showed me how Elijah was intimidated by Jezebel. I finally recognized that my behavior was exactly what this intimidating, discouraging spirit wanted. It wanted me to back off from what God sent me to do.

I immediately went after the root of the symptoms I had struggled with all day—a spirit of intimidation. I boldly broke free and felt released from confusion and frustration.

How to Break the Spirit of Intimidation

So, if intimidation lulls the gift asleep, what wakes us up? The answer: *boldness*. Intimidation causes a person to draw back, while boldness lunges forward even in the face of opposition. How can an intimidated person apprehend boldness? "For God has not given us a spirit of fear [intimidation], but of power and of love and of a sound mind" (2 Tim. 1:7, NKJV).

Boldness comes from the virtues of power, love, and soundness of mind. Boldness is not a virtue in itself. We have all known people who were brazen and bold. True boldness comes from God and is fueled by godly virtue. Boldness that is fueled by God's character awakens the gifts in our lives.

Some people do not have virtue behind their boldness. They know the right things to say and act confident when faced with little or no opposition. But their strength does not run deep. It is superficial. Their bold face is a mask for arrogance or ignorance. Their roots are shallow, and eventually a strong enough storm will expose them. When the weather is good, you can't see how deeply a tree is rooted, but under the winds of adversity it will either be uprooted or proven strong.

David said, "The LORD is the strength of my life; of whom shall I be afraid?" (Ps. 27:1, NKJV). David declared the Lord as his source of strength and power. Knowing there is none greater than God, he could fearlessly declare, "I fear no one!"

Not only did he boldly declare his confidence, but he lived it as well. David knew the power of God because he knew God. This boldness enabled him to fulfill his destiny and rule righteously. David's boldness was so contagious that Israel's hope was restored.

Let's look at how power, love, and a sound mind produced the boldness David needed to withstand any intimidation he faced.

1. Power. He knew God, and he knew that God was greater and more powerful than anything David would face.

2. Love. He loved God more than himself.

3. A sound mind. He would not be moved until he had the word or mind of the Lord, no matter how great the pressure.

When our spirits are filled with power, love, and the word of the Lord, we will not fall prey to intimidation. It is not just one of these virtues but the combination of all three that undergirds us. Paul would have listed only one if that was all it took. To walk in godly boldness, it takes all three.

Chapter 7

GAIN CONFIDENCE THROUGH INTIMACY WITH GOD

One thing I have desired of the LORD, that will I seek: that I may dwell in the house of the LORD all the days of my life, to behold the beauty of the LORD, and to inquire in His temple.

—PSALM 27:4, NKJV

IN THE WILDERNESS of Judea, just after John baptized Jesus at the Jordan River, the heavens opened and the voice of the Lord broke forth. As Jesus came up out of the water, the Spirit of God descended on Him like a dove, and His Father leaned over the balcony of heaven to say, "This is My beloved Son, in whom I am well pleased" (Matt. 3:17, NKJV). With this thunderous statement the Father prepared His Son's heart to enter into one of the great tests of His earthly life—the temptation of Satan in the wilderness.*

Scripture records only three occasions when God the Father spoke to Jesus audibly. This was one of them. It

---

* Mike Bickle, *After God's Own Heart* (Lake Mary, FL: Charisma House, 2009), 215–216, 218, 223, 227.

is highly significant to us that just before Jesus encountered Satan personally in Matthew 4, the Father renewed the sense of connection and intimacy between Father and Son. Though Jesus is fully God, in His humanity He needed refreshing. He was not automatically strengthened, but, like us, He grew physically and mentally weary. And so this is a pattern for how God the Father deals with us. As Jesus faced the daunting task ahead of Him in the wilderness, the voice of His Father reassured Him of the greatest privilege given the human race: that we enjoy intimacy with the Godhead. This intimacy empowered Jesus to face the trials of the enemy, and this same intimacy equips us to overcome the trials of life. Indeed, this assurance of our special closeness to God is the only thing that can equip and prepare our hearts for this crucial hour in history, when great revival and the greatest divine judgments are about to break forth. I'm convinced that just as the Father spoke strength to Jesus by expressing His delight in Him, so God will empower us by assuring us of His delight in us.

What is the path to overcoming great fear in the end times? The examples of Jesus and David make it clear: they overcame fear by seeking God's face in intimacy. They gazed upon the heart of God, encountering His beauty. David wrote:

> One thing I have desired of the LORD, that will I seek: that I may dwell in the house of the LORD all the days of my life, to behold the beauty of the LORD, and to inquire in His temple. For in the time of trouble He shall hide me in His pavilion;

in the secret place of His tabernacle shall He hide me.... And now my head shall be lifted up above my enemies all around me.... Hear, O LORD, when I cry with my voice! Have mercy also upon me, and answer me. When You said, "Seek My face," my heart said to You, "Your face, LORD, will I seek."

—PSALM 27:4–8, NKJV

Fear will not go away by itself; we have to rise up and resist it. To uplift his heart and overcome the darkness of fear, David prophesied, "Though an army may encamp against me, my heart shall not fear; though war may rise against me, in this I will be confident" (Ps. 27:3, NKJV). David decided that whenever his heart started wavering, he would move to a place of communion with God instead of caving under the weight of the attack. We must do our part of the division of labor when fear comes. We are not to just endure it. We must arise in confidence and assert the opposite of what fear is telling us.

David would have lost all hope if he hadn't known that sooner or later he would experience a breakthrough of God's goodness. God usually hides the breakthrough until it comes. We can't always see it coming. Then *bam!* It hits. Until then we have to aggressively press in to God's beauty. David put it this way: "Wait on the LORD; be of good courage, and He shall strengthen your heart" (Ps. 27:14, NKJV). We don't wilt on the side of the road. Rather, we pray courageously, seek His face diligently, and stand firm with what we know to be true. Our souls will be anchored in the unchanging, unyielding love of God. We will experience the promise Jesus made to His disciples: "I am with you always, even to the end of the age" (Matt. 28:20, NKJV). This promise is for intimacy and nearness. It will sustain our hearts.

Chapter 8

OVERCOMING PANIC
WITH THE WORD

Whenever I am afraid, I will trust in You.
In God (I will praise His word), in God I
have put my trust; I will not fear.

—PSALM 56:3–4, NKJV

O NE OF THE devil's decisions for your life is to get you
to panic and to begin bouncing around emotionally,
this way and that, like a rubber ball. He wants you so con-
fused and mixed up that you don't know who you are or
how to handle the situation you're in.*

I get excited because I know what the Word of God is
able to do for me. The Word can preach power into me.
I've been sick, and the Word of God has preached sickness
out of my body. I've been discouraged, and it preached discouragement out of my mind. I have suffered from panic
attacks, and the Word of God preached the panic attacks
out of my life.

---

* Mike Purkey, *Reversing the Devil's Decision* (Lake Mary, FL: Charisma
House, 2000), 160–162; 171–172.

If you struggle with panic and fear, you need to follow Paul's advice:

> Finally, brethren, whatever things are true, whatever things are noble, whatever things are just, whatever things are pure, whatever things are lovely, whatever things are of good report, if there is any virtue and if there is anything praiseworthy—meditate on these things.
>
> —PHILIPPIANS 4:8, NKJV

You don't get rid of negative, panicky thoughts by trying not to think about them; you overcome them by continually choosing the truth until the negative thoughts are overwhelmed by the power of the truth.

Do you remember when you were a child trying to sleep through a storm? Every time the thunder crashed or a tree branch tapped against your window, you knew the world was coming to an end. If you dared to look out the window, you were sure you could see the boogeyman trying to break into your house. But as an adult, watching a storm can be exciting because it displays the awesome power of God.

In the same way, when the storm hits, you can hear the crashing and make the choice to believe that your world is coming to an end, or you can sit back and enjoy watching an awesome display of the power of God.

When the children of Israel were trapped between the Red Sea and the oncoming Egyptian army—a storm if there ever was one—God spoke:

Fear not; stand still (firm, confident, undismayed) and see the salvation of the Lord which He will work for you today.

—Exodus 14:13, AMP

The devil hides in the shadows. He dwells in the realm of imaginations. He feeds on fear. And to act on that fear—to panic—is to act as if Satan is bigger that God. But once we realize that our fear is

- F—alse
- E—vidence
- A—ppearing
- R—eal,

we understand that what we are afraid of may not even exist at all. But even if it *is* real, our God is bigger. Because Jesus defeated death and the grave, no power on earth is stronger.

The greatest battles being fought today are not on the battlefield of foreign wars; they're fought in the minds of men and women. The battle *you* fight against panic will take place in *your* mind. You must be consistent—you must continually feed on the Word. You must believe it and act on it.

At the same time you can't expect to hear the Word and not obey it and then when the storm hits, to successfully stand against it. You can prepare to overcome panic by acting NOW! Obey the Word NOW! Do what it says NOW! Then when the storm comes, your foundation will be strong and the power of God's Word will strengthen you to stand firm until the storm has passed and all is peaceful once more.

Chapter 9

DOES JESUS CARE
WHEN WE ARE AFRAID?

Cast all your anxiety on him because he cares for you.
—1 Peter 5:7, niv

Josif Tson has pointed out that the phrase "fear not" (or its equivalent) is found 366 times in the Bible—one for every day of the year and an extra one for leap year! God does not want us to be afraid.*

You may have a problem so terrifying, but it is too sensitive to discuss with another—even your best friend. It is good if you *can* discuss it with another, at least your minister, but never, never, never doubt that our Lord Jesus cares, understands, accepts, loves, and gives strength and guidance. One caution: don't wear the mask with Him. Nothing could be more foolish. He knows all anyway! "All things are naked and opened unto the eyes of him with whom we have to do" (Heb. 4:13, kjv). Our heavenly Father knows what you need even before you ask Him (Matt. 6:8).

---

* R. T. Kendall, *The Unfailing Love of Jesus* (Lake Mary, FL: Charisma House, 2008), 42, 48–50, 52–53, 55–57.

Don't play the game with God. Unburden your heart to Him. Tell Him *everything*. Hide absolutely nothing. You will find that He does not scold, laugh, moralize, or rebuke. He is touched. Hallelujah, what a God!

Are you afraid? Jesus understands. But do not be surprised if our Lord will not allow you to run from your problem. He accepts us as we are—not because He approves, but because He knows we need Him and all the help He can give us.

But we must be willing to let Him help us. We must not hide or run from the problem by retreating to darkness. In many years of being a pastor, I have learned this: most people don't want their problems solved. They want them understood. The thing is, I might understand your problem; I might not. But in any case, I cannot help those who do not want help.

Jesus accepts us that He might teach us repentance. We must come openly before Him and be utterly willing to walk in the light He gives. God does not lead us directly from A to Z, but from A to B, B to C, etc. Ask God to lead you to B.

The marvel is, He *does* understand. Many people come to me whose problems I don't understand. But our Lord is one who understands and sympathizes with *every* problem. I can sympathize with one who has lost a mother or who may have had a traumatic experience in the dark as a child. There are certainly many other areas in which I can sympathize with those who have needs. But with Jesus, we have One who is totally sympathetic with every problem— tempted in *every* way that we are.

He Will Meet All Your Needs

The fear of insecurity is dealt with by our walking in the light (1 John 1:7). In the Sermon on the Mount Jesus upbraided men for the fear of want. It was a command that you should "not worry about your life, what you will eat or drink; or about your body, what you will wear" (Matt. 6:25, NIV). Paul said that the "love of money is a root of all kinds of evil" (1 Tim. 6:10, NIV). Many of us like to think we are exempt from the love of money merely because we do not expect (or want) to live in luxury. But the fear of whether or not our needs will be supplied springs from the same bitter well.

The task of the Christian is to walk in the light and develop faith to the degree that our obedience to Christ is *never* in jeopardy of owing to financial considerations. When God tells us to "go," we must *move*. Once we begin to lag behind due to fear of how our need will be supplied, the devil will slip in, and—before we know it—we shall have completely rationalized away God's call.

The fear of insecurity needs to be dealt with in a radical manner. "And my God will meet *all your needs* according to his glorious riches in Christ Jesus" (Phil. 4:19, NIV, emphasis added). My father's favorite verse is: "But seek first his kingdom and his righteousness, and all these things will be given to you as well" (Matt. 6:33, NIV). As long as Satan can succeed in tempting us to worry about financial and material things, our discipleship will never rise above second class. "No one who puts his hand to the plow and looks back is fit for service in the kingdom of God" (Luke 9:62, NIV).

We must walk in the day. No fear of man. No fear of insecurity. There must be a trust that the same God who supplied the need in the past will do it again.

Does Jesus care when we are afraid? Yes, He cares. But He makes us face fear and gives us the power and strength to do so.

We can overcome the fear of man by confessing Christ and witnessing for Him—anywhere.

We can overcome the fear of insecurity by seeking His glory first and then trusting Him to supply every need. He will do it!

We can overcome the fear of death by acknowledging our sinfulness and Christ's deity and right to rule us, pleading nothing but the blood that He shed on the cross, repenting of our sins, and giving Him our lives. Great peace will follow when you do this from your very heart.

Does Jesus care when we are afraid? Yes. He understands. By accepting us as we are, He can bring us to be what He is—a man of faith, of courage. God wants to do that for you.

Chapter 10

RUN *TO* THE ROAR

Resist the devil and he will flee from you.

—JAMES 4:7, NKJV

T HE PEOPLE ARE quite nervous," said Maritz, a sea-soned safari guide and a Christian. He had accompa-nied us on our trip to this small village in the African bush and introduced us to the people. Maritz had long flowing locks of curly hair. A big man, he exuded power. "Four renegade lions have broken through the predator fence and have killed seven or eight people. Everyone is afraid." Now I understood the people's mood that night.*

In spite of the tension and grief that tempered the eve-ning, nearly everyone in the village gathered to view the *JESUS* film we had brought. Once I had the film rolling, I moved to the back of the crowd where Maritz and mem-bers of the mission team stood near the fence conversing quietly. The subject, of course, was *lions.*

---

* Joe Hurston and Martha VanCise, *Run to the Roar* (Lake Mary, FL: Charisma House, 2006), 2–6.

"If I hear a lion roar, you'll see me running," one young man said.

"*Never run from a lion,*" Maritz said quietly. "Run to the roar."

"Do what!" I said.

"Run to the roar."

"Everything inside me would say, 'Run away from the roar,'" I said. The others nodded their heads in agreement.

"You want to know where that lion is," Maritz explained. "You don't want to be running blindly through the bush or through the village when a lion roars. If it's roaring, it has probably already seen you. That lion can run faster than you can. You don't want it to overtake you from behind while you're running blindly in fear. You need to go toward the roar in order to figure out where the lion is and then plan your escape. If you take a direct approach to the roar, all your senses will be tuned to finding out where the lion is located. Then you can maneuver away from the lion and escape."

Maritz could run to the roar, but I scanned the area looking for a good hiding place if a lion showed up.

The Lion Rules Vast Territories by Intimidation

A lion's roar can be heard for five miles. The circle of intimidation covers a large area. The apostle Peter said that the devil prowled like a roaring lion looking for someone to devour (1 Pet. 5:8). As you near any accomplishment, you will hear the lion roar. "Failure! Failure! You can't come here! Give up! Give up! It can't be done." But the lion lies and exaggerates his power. (See John 8:44). I won't deny that the roar has made my heart pound, but God's ever-present enabling has given me boldness to resist and overcome many lions. Have I always been victorious in every lion confrontation? If your idea of victory is standing unscathed with one foot on the lion's head—well, no, I haven't always been victorious. If your concept of victory is bearing the scars of conflict but still being committed to following the Guide through lion territory—the answer is yes.

When you enter the kingdom of heaven, you also enter lion territory. Programs emphasizing "celebrate Jesus" and "God wants you to be happy" often grow churches, but they fail to prepare the Christian for the realities of lion-infested country. Celebrate that your name has been entered in the Lamb's Book of Life; be aware, though, that your name has been penciled on the lion's menu as *"soup de jour."*

The lion disguises himself in discouragement, unfavorable circumstances, and unsolvable problems. When encountering these situations you can ignore them, retreat, or move toward the difficulty. The apostle Peter, who turned his back and ran at one lion encounter, tells us to resist the lion and to stand firm (1 Pet. 5:9). With the boldness of God empowering you, you can run to the roar, facing head-on your fears, problems, and adversities that block your path, and accomplish God's purpose for your life.

—◎◎ **PART 3** ◎◎—

HOPE DURING
LIFE'S CHALLENGES

Chapter 11

A GOOD GOD CAN BRING GOOD THINGS OUT OF BAD TIMES

You intended to harm me, but God intended it for good to accomplish what is now being done, the saving of many lives.

—GENESIS 50:20, NIV

EVERY PERSON WALKS through valleys, those places of difficulty and suffering where we feel lonely, God-forsaken, and hurt. In the valleys, fear and doubt become our traveling companions. Some valleys are deeper and longer than others, perhaps caused by the death of a child or a loved one. Others are shorter and more manageable, more of a hassle than a genuine hardship. Some bring on a mild case of the blues; others are so painful that we yearn to die.*

Life has a way of beating us up—no matter how much faith we have, no matter what spiritual camp we are in, no matter how many demons we cast out or how many "words from the Lord" we receive. Even for the believer, then, life

---

* Jim Reeve, *God Never Wastes a Hurt* (Lake Mary, FL: Charisma House, 2000), 2–5.

is a mixture of pain and pleasure, victory and defeat, success and failure, mountain peaks and valleys. We are not bad people merely because we are experiencing stress and frustration. We are simply people. Welcome to the human race!

Every one of us has hidden hurts that no one else knows about. A woman told me once, "When I walked up the aisle to marry the man of my dreams and start a new life, I didn't realize how much emotional baggage was underneath my beautiful makeup and white dress." Because we carry these wounds with us wherever we go, neither new surroundings nor new relationships bring the relief we so long for. Neither a brave smile nor a stiff upper lip can remove the reality that all of us have bumps, scrapes, and bruises. And the sooner we become honest about this, the sooner we can discover our way out.

Valleys are nothing new, nor are the particular problems we face today all that different from the problems of yesterday. The Bible alludes to several of life's valleys that are as real today as they were thousands of years ago, including:

- The valley of calamity (Josh. 7:26)
- The valley of giants (Josh. 15:8)
- The valley of weeping (Ps. 84:6)
- The valley of dry bones (Ezek. 37:1)
- The valley of the shadow of death (Ps. 23)

Of all the valleys in the Bible, probably the most well known is the one found in Psalm 23. Because at one time or another all of us must face our own mortality, the beautifully poetic words of this passage touch saint and sinner alike. I have been in hospitals chatting with unabashed non-Christians who were lying in their deathbeds, and they have surprised me by reciting from memory this psalm. Maybe it is only a vague recollection from their childhood or a lasting remnant of something their mother taught them. From whatever source, in response to my asking them if they knew anything about the Bible, they quietly start quoting: "The LORD is my shepherd; I shall not want.... Yea, though I walk through the valley of the shadow of death, I will fear no evil: for thou art with me" (Ps. 23:1, 4, KJV).

I suspect nonbelievers somehow have a sense, perhaps a persistent hope, that help is available even while facing the deepest and darkest of valleys. It is told how W. C. Fields, the famous comedian of early cinema and an avowed atheist, was "caught" reading the Bible on his deathbed. With his stereotyped comedic voice, he said, "Looking for loopholes."

David wrote the Twenty-Third Psalm from personal experience. Sheep were safe with David, no matter where their journeys took them. He cared for his flock, keeping them healthy and well fed. If necessary, he protected them. David had risked his own life for his flock, killing a lion and bear on two separate occasions using only his bare hands. David had been a good shepherd to his sheep, but more importantly he knew that he too had a Good Shepherd watching over him, no matter where his journeys took him.

David had an unrelenting belief that God was good. This conviction sustained him during those times when life seemed anything but good. There is an old Arab proverb that says, "All sunshine and no rain make a desert." This is not simply a case of "when life give you lemons, make lemonade," but rather a sense that just maybe a good God can bring good things out of bad times. David knew that valleys were not just something to *go* through, but to *grow* through.

I have traveled to Israel and visited a valley called the Valley of the Shadow of Death. Whether or not this is the valley that David was referring to, we don't know, but the canyon is so narrow and deep that the sun shines on the floor for only moments a day. The rest of the time the canyon is covered in shadows, sometimes very dark shadows.

Many of us are in valleys like that. A valley to David would be like a dark alley to us. All the fear and danger associated with an alley—that's what David meant. We have all seen TV shows where a woman gets off work late in a bad part of town and decides to take a shortcut to her car through an alleyway. Invariably something bad happens, and she has to run from some sort of lowlife she bumped into there.

God says that even if we find ourselves in one of those situations, we do not have to fear evil.

Are you going through a tough time? Do you feel as if your life is falling apart? That is a valley, and life is full of them. Don't despair! Millions have been through them, and you too will emerge better, stronger, and healthier than you went in. God will not waste that valley, but He will raise you up to a high place to teach others what you have learned.

Chapter 12

A WINNING STRATEGY
FOR VICTORY

Thanks be to God, who gives us
victory through our Lord Jesus Christ.

—1 Corinthians 15:57, nkjv

T HE WINNING STRATEGY for becoming victorious over life's
challenges involves following the Lord wholly, yielding to
the Holy Spirit at every point where your will, your thoughts,
and your desires differ with His divine purpose for your life.
The Holy Spirit comes to dwell in your spirit, filling you with
the life of God. He will express that divine life through your
soul—your mind, your emotions and will.*

When God's will becomes your will, His thoughts your
thoughts, and His desires your desires, you can say with the
apostle Paul:

> I have been crucified with Christ; and it is no longer
> I who live, but Christ lives in me; and the life which

---

* Fuchsia Pickett, *Possess Your Promised Land* (Lake Mary, FL: Charisma
House, 2003), 94, 101–104.

I now live in the flesh I live by faith in the Son of
God, who loved me and gave Himself up for me.
—GALATIANS 2:20, NAS

Surrender: The Key to Conquest

God is faithful to exchange your sinful nature for His divine
nature as you determine to bring your self-life to the cross.
A. B. Simpson asks and answers these important questions:

> How shall we overcome these giants? How shall we
> win the victory over self? We must surrender our-
> selves so utterly that we can never own ourselves
> again. We must hand over self and all its rights
> in an eternal covenant, and give God the absolute
> right to own us, control us and possess us forever.
> We must let God make this real in detail, as each
> day brings its tests and conflicts. We must receive
> the great antidote to self—the love of Christ. And
> finally, we need not only the love of Christ but
> Christ Himself. It is not a principle, nor an emo-
> tion, not a motive, that is to transform our life and
> conquer these determined foes, but it is a living
> Person.[1]

Christ has made it possible for you to lose your self-life
as you become a partaker of His divine nature. The apostle
Peter declared this truth triumphantly:

> …His divine power has granted to us everything
> pertaining to life and godliness, through the true
> knowledge of Him who called us by His own glory

and excellence. For by these He has granted to us His precious and magnificent promises, so that by them you may become partakers of the divine nature, having escaped the corruption that is in the world by lust.

—2 Peter 1:2–4, NAS

Living victoriously involves the ability to live a holy life and receive impartation of the divine nature as you continually give yourself to God and learn to truly know Him. He makes it possible for you to become a partaker of the divine nature, delivering you from the corruption of this generation. As you study His Word, humbly seeking Him, you will begin to think as He thinks; you will exchange your worldly thoughts for His kingdom thoughts.

The Holy Spirit will cause the written Word to live in you, and Christ, who is the Word, will become your life. You will realize the reality of what the apostle Paul wrote: "Christ in you, the hope of glory" (Col. 1:27, NAS). As I wrote in my book *Placed in His Glory:*

> The work of the Holy Spirit is to reveal the glory of Jesus in us. As long as we are in control, He can't be. The "I" nature wants to rule, having my way and exercising my rights, never allowing the Holy Spirit to do what He came to do. If we take our "I" to the cross, we can exchange it there for the I AM. Then the Holy Spirit moves into every area of our personality, and the veil of flesh begins to fall away. We begin to realize that we don't think as we used to think. The truth will dawn on us: "These aren't my thoughts." Then we understand Paul's injunction to

"Let this mind be in you which was also in Christ Jesus" (Phil. 2:5)....

The Holy Spirit begins to replace Adam's carnal mind with the mind of Christ so we can think as our Daddy thinks. Then He changes our rebellious wills as well. As we keep surrendering to the Holy Spirit, He begins to take the Father's will that we know nothing about and move into our wills. He makes our wills His will and His will our will, if we say yes to Him. As we yield to the Holy Spirit's work within us, we begin to walk with God and to become the will of God.[2]

Perhaps you will never fully grasp the wonder of redemption, even throughout all of eternity. But you can rejoice in it and experience the reality of the life of Christ in you as you abandon yourself to the Holy Spirit within you. He has come to change you into the image of Christ, causing this "treasure in earthen vessels" to shine forth, "that the excellency of the power may be of God, and not of us" (2 Cor. 4:7, KJV). And He made your victory possible:

When you were dead in your transgressions and the uncircumcision of your flesh, He made you alive together with Him, having forgiven us all our transgressions, having canceled out the certificate of debt consisting of decrees against us, which was hostile to us; and He has taken it out of the way, having nailed it to the cross. When He had disarmed the rulers

and authorities, He made a public display of them,
having triumphed over them through Him.

—COLOSSIANS 2:13–15, NAS

Christ did it all for us. We have the power through a sur-
rendered life in Him to defeat our enemies and be victorious!

Chapter 13

BREAK FREE FROM NEGATIVE EMOTIONS DURING HARD TIMES

Why are you downcast, O my soul? Why so disturbed within me? Put your hope in God, for I will yet praise him, my savior and my God.

—PSALM 42:5–6, NIV

ANY NUMBER OF things can easily affect our feelings. What we have eaten, how well we have slept, what time of the month it is, whether the man or woman in our life has recently and sincerely kissed us, how many times the phone has rung while we have been trying to prepare dinner, and the list goes on.*

When you have come under a tyranny of negative feelings and someone tells you to focus on something else for a little while until your emotions have settled or you've "calmed down," it makes you feel angry and rejected, doesn't it? You feel as if the person doesn't understand the problem or doesn't accept you. The person has "questioned the validity"

---

* Paula Sandford, *Healing for a Woman's Emotions* (Lake Mary, FL: Charisma House, 2007), 99–101, 110–111, 116.

of your perceptions. You perceive it as lack of respect for the way you feel, and it hurts you even more.

Because you have exalted your personal feelings as *truth*, you defend and nurse your feelings, and therefore these feelings easily take you captive. When someone suggests a need to relax, that a situation might not warrant such intensity, you often feel accused. How often have you said or heard someone say:

- "What? You don't think I ought to feel upset?"

- "Wouldn't you be upset if that had happened to you?"

- "You're saying there is something wrong with me!"

You have only two alternatives: you can hide or deny your feelings, plus suppress them and wallow in them, or you can exalt your feelings, insist, persist—and wallow! More often than not, we usually do the latter. But even if you choose denial, it is only a matter of time before the pressure of what has been suppressed increases to the point of an eruption. The wallowing time is what has increased the force of the explosion, whereas had you not believed and nurtured your feelings, time would have brought balance and rest.

Few who exalt their feelings can successfully shut them down, but those who are successful in turning off their emotions most often also lose the capacity to feel the positive emotions that enable a person to experience zest for life. You can spiral into depression from either direction.

Let Your Feelings Live!

Everyone has feelings. *The important thing is what we learn to do with them.* We should allow our feelings to live. Even though they often fail to represent objective truth, they are good indicators of what has lodged in our hearts. But we are in trouble if our minds make decisions solely based upon what we are feeling. Our hearts' emotions were not intended to rule our minds and direct our actions. Mark 7:21–23 says, "For from *within*, out of the *heart* of men, proceed the evil thoughts, fornications, thefts, murders, adulteries, deeds of coveting and wickedness, as well as deceit, sensuality, envy, slander, pride and foolishness. All these evil things proceed from *within* and defile the man" (NAS, emphasis added).

In other words, we are to be *renewed* in the spirit of our *minds* (Eph. 4:23). With the renewed mind we may instruct our hearts in what to do with the emotions we feel, how to act, and how to "put on the new self, created to be like God in *true* righteousness and holiness" (Eph. 4:24, NIV, emphasis added).

As we surrender our emotions to God, He will renew our minds through His Word. He will show us the right balance in our responses to life's difficulties. How will this happen? We must walk in a discipline:

1. Die to our demands

2. Choose to forgive when others treat us insensitively

3. Tell God immediately about a slight or injury before the emotion has a chance to lodge in our hearts

4. Ask God for the best way to respond

Such a discipline is necessarily a daily business. Paul said, "*I die daily*" (1 Cor. 15:31, NAS, emphasis added).

> I *have been crucified* with Christ; and it is no longer I who live, but Christ lives in me; and the life which I now live in the flesh I live by faith in the Son of God, who loved me and gave Himself up for me.
>
> —GALATIANS 2:20, NAS,
> EMPHASIS ADDED

What emotional balance and rest we can enjoy when we have acknowledged, confessed, and crucified our patterns of natural response to life's problems!

Chapter 14

A SACRIFICE OF PRAISE

Through Jesus, therefore, let us continually
offer to God a sacrifice of praise—the
fruit of lips that confess his name.

—HEBREWS 13:15, NIV

IT IS NOT often I get a new flash of insight when I am actually preaching. I wish I did, for there's nothing quite like it for a preacher. Most of my insights come when I am working fairly hard in preparation. But one evening when I was preaching on John 11, the Holy Spirit quickened me as I read John 11:14–15, "So then he told them plainly, Lazarus is dead, and for your sake I am glad I was not there, so that you may believe" (NIV).*

The nearest we ever got to the problem of evil is the truth inherent in John 11:15. The eternal problem of evil—"Why does God allow evil and suffering?"—is unanswerable and unknowable in this life. It is the hardest of all. If people think they are clever because they suddenly come up with this heavy question, "If God is all-powerful but

---

* R. T. Kendall, *Just Say Thanks!* (Lake Mary, FL: Charisma House, 2005), 56, 58–61, 63.

67

all-merciful, why does He allow suffering?", they should realize it is for their sake that they don't get the answer. God does us a favor—an infinite favor—by not answering this ancient theological-philosophical question.

In a word: God doesn't answer our questions for our sake. It is a mercy. It means we still have an opportunity to believe—to demonstrate true faith. For God chose to decree that people will be saved by faith alone or be eternally lost. He wants a people who trust Him on the basis of His Word, not the outward evidence. He desires a people who rely on Him without getting all their questions answered, even a people who believe Him when He doesn't seem to make sense.

One day God will clear His name. He will do it so brilliantly and totally and conclusively that our mouths will be forever stopped. It will be the total vindication of God Himself. But it will also mean everlasting destruction for those who wait until then to get their questions answered. For seeing is not believing.

This tells me that when I am low and sad and facing a future with anxiety, I have a wonderful opportunity to believe! This is now—right now—I can really please God. "And without faith it is impossible to please God, because anyone who comes to him must believe that he exists and that he rewards those who earnestly seek him" (Heb. 11:6, NIV).

Praising God when I am sad pleases Him. It shows I trust His Word and that I love Him without His doing everything that pleases me. It is a wonderful opportunity for blessing—just to believe!

It is also called a "sacrifice of praise" (Heb. 13:15, NIV). This is because it is a sacrifice to praise God when we don't feel like it. We sacrifice feelings, we sacrifice pleasure, we sacrifice time—just to praise God. And when we don't feel like it—when we are at a low point, we then really show a sacrifice of praise. In fact, the lower we are, the greater the opportunity to demonstrate a sacrifice of praise to God. This is why God was pleased when Job said, "Though he slay me, yet will I hope in him" (Job 13:15, NIV).

Paul said, "Therefore, I urge you, brothers, in view of God's mercy, to offer your bodies as living sacrifices, holy and pleasing to God—this is your spiritual act of worship" (Rom. 12:1, NIV). Peter said we offer "spiritual sacrifices acceptable to God through Jesus Christ" (1 Pet. 2:5, NIV). Paul deemed his gifts from the Philippians as a "fragrant offering, an acceptable sacrifice, pleasing to God" (Phil. 4:18, NIV). David said, "I will sacrifice a thank offering to you and call on the name of the LORD" (Ps. 116:17, NIV).

When we take the time to praise God, we sacrifice time. We all can think of things we ought to be doing. It is easier to watch television than it is to take the equal amount of time to praise God. Which is easier—to watch *Frasier* for thirty minutes or to praise God for thirty minutes? To praise God for thirty minutes is a sacrifice of time, of pleasure, of our basic wishes, and, possibly, of our temperament. It isn't easy!

But when we are low, the outlook is bleak, and when we are anxious, it is doubly hard to praise God. But God likes it. I believe it pleases Him more than ever; He sees what we feel, what we are giving up and struggling to do.

Are you low at this moment as you read these lines? This chapter is for you. And if you are not feeling so depressed or anxious at present, I predict that you may well need to recall this in the future! It is only a matter of time before we will be faced with a trial and with uncertainty. Paul said, "So that no one would be unsettled by these trials. You know quite well that we were destined for them" (1 Thess. 3:3, NIV). "For it has been granted to you on behalf of Christ not only to believe on him, but also to suffer for him" (Phil. 1:29, NIV). "I ask you, therefore, not to be discouraged because of my sufferings for you, which are your glory" (Eph. 3:13, NIV).

While in the process of writing this, I woke up one morning with vertigo—a state of dizziness, which gave me difficulty walking. I am not sure what caused it. I tried hard to read my Bible and pray through my prayer lists. Louise and our daughter, Melissa, laid their hands on me and prayed. Sadly, I didn't feel much better.

It was a Saturday that this happened. I had to be at Westminster Chapel for our Pilot Light ministry. On the same day Christian Deaf Link was using the premises of the Chapel, and I had been asked to address them. I was fighting self-pity as I struggled to get there.

But then I found myself feeling so ashamed when I watched a hundred deaf people singing. Not that I heard them, for I could hardly hear a sound as they were singing with sign language. It was amazing. The young lady who led them was almost being carried away by her joy of what she was feeling. I realized how fortunate I was to be able to hear and to speak. My vertigo had diminished a bit, but it was in any case a far cry from having no hearing and no voice—only the ability to sing in sign language. I thought to myself, "If these people can praise God with their handicap, I most certainly can do the same with this feeling of dizziness—a temporary condition that could not compare with their disability." I determined to rejoice and praise and thank God. I didn't much feel like it, but I felt I had so much to be thankful for.

Chapter 15

COUNT IT ALL JOY

My brethren, count it all joy when you
fall into various trials, knowing that the
testing of your faith produces patience.
—JAMES 1:2–3, NKJV

COUNTING IT PURE joy to face the fact of my natural
lack of brilliance is what I have to do for many years.*
I know also that people often laugh or roll their eyes heav-
enward when they hear me talk like this, as many think I
am far more gifted than I really am. They don't know that
it is the Holy Spirit who has managed to break through to
me because I need unusual help, and that I have received
such help because God managed to make me more teach-
able. God chose not to give me the brain of a John Calvin
or a Jonathan Edwards; neither did He give me the oratory
of a Charles Spurgeon or a Martyn Lloyd-Jones. And yet
He chose to give me a respectable platform from which to
preach! What was I to do? I chose to count my insufficiency

---

* R. T. Kendall, *Pure Joy* (Lake Mary, FL: Charisma House, 2006), 14–15,
21–22, 27–32.

for these things pure joy in order that God would use me—not to mention get the glory.

What the King James Version translates as "count" it all joy in James 1:2–3, the New International Version translates as "consider" it pure joy. The Greek word is *heegeomai*; it means "to value highly, to esteem." Paul used this when he said to King Agrippa, "I consider myself fortunate to stand before you today" (Acts 26:2, NIV). Moses "regarded" disgrace for the sake of Christ as of greater value than the treasures of Egypt because he was looking ahead to his reward (Heb. 11:26).

We therefore are to consider having to face trials of many kinds as pure joy. *Trial* is thus a word often used in an ironic sense. What would naturally make us feel the opposite—to be upset or feel sorry for ourselves—is to be taken as a wonderful privilege, or opportunity, instead.

Who enjoys the feeling of disgrace? It would, after all, be abnormal to enjoy this. Unless, that is, one had a definite reason for feeling this way. Moses did. He considered disgrace as more valuable than earthly luxury—all because it put him in a good place for the future. Jesus endured the cross because of the joy set before Him (Heb. 12:2). The apostle Paul used *heegeomai* when he referred to the "pluses" of his background—being circumcised the eighth day, being of the stock of Israel and of the tribe of Benjamin, being a Pharisee, and faultless as to legalistic righteousness. He considered these things not pluses but minuses—all because of the dazzling privilege of knowing Jesus. That is simply the way he regarded those things that most people would love (Phil. 3:5–8).

This is what James wants us to do when we face trials

of many kinds: consider them pure joy. It doesn't make sense, and yet it does! He tells us to consider trials as pure joy because of what they do for us if we believe and apply these words. It will be seen to make very good sense indeed. James wants us to see it now—by faith. Moses did what he did—regarding disgrace for the sake of Jesus of inestimable value—by faith, and he was never sorry he made that choice. Neither will any of us be.

Yet it is not easy to do this. James puts a task before us that is exceedingly difficult.

But we must realize that perseverance is the ultimate goal. It is what enables you to reach the goal that James envisages: "Perseverance must finish its work so that you may be mature and complete, not lacking anything" (James 1:4, NIV). This means a peace and contentment so vast and so profound that you no longer crave what you once thought was so important to you. "The LORD is my shepherd; I shall not want" (Ps. 23:1, KJV). James sees a time ahead for the person who dignifies the trial that will mean indescribable peace, the highest level of anointing, the soul uncluttered by greed, and a heart filled with the very presence of God. It is pure joy.

In other words, if you consider a trial to be pure joy, it will lead to pure joy. Count it pure joy, call it pure joy, regard the trial as pure joy, and one day you will experience pure joy for yourself. I promise it!

So when a trial comes your way

1. Welcome it—for it comes with one purpose: for your own good.

2. Don't panic—"it leads only to evil" (Ps. 37:8, NIV).

3. See the trial as a compliment to you from God Himself.

4. Never forget that God allowed it.

5. Know that there is a purpose in it.

6. Don't try to end it. Let God do this so that you derive the full benefit of His grace.

7. Don't grumble. It takes great grace to endure the hard times.

8. Know that God wants you to pass the test far more than you do.

PART 4

HOPE IN LOVE

Chapter 16

LOVE IS ALWAYS ENOUGH

Though I bestow all my goods to feed the poor, and
though I give my body to be burned, but have not love,
it profits me nothing.... The greatest of these is love.

—1 CORINTHIANS 13:3, 13, NKJV

I FELT ANGRY. I did not understand why God would give us 320 children and then allow them to be beaten up and made homeless. I knew theologically that Father God loved us and loved these children, but I surely did not understand how to be a peacemaker in the midst of it all.*

I remember looking into the faces of the children one by one, trying to think what would bring them hope. Since the first day I had picked them up from the streets, I had taught the children, "We must love without limit. We will love without end."

A friend of mine named Manessa, who had been a soldier during the war, was very protective of me. One day, when a twenty-dollar contract was put out on my life, he came to me and said, "Don't worry, Mama Aida. I have a

---

* Heidi Baker, *Compelled by Love* (Lake Mary, FL: Charisma House, 2008), 110–112.

plan!" He promised to protect me. He told me he had an AK-47 and grenade under his bed. He said, "I will go and kill them for you."

Manessa thought I would be very happy to hear of his offer to me, but I turned to him and said, "We are here to love and to bring peace."

I made a decision to go back to the center in broad daylight. I knew the danger to my life, but I wanted to speak to my village friends about love and forgiveness. I shared my heart with them and told them, "I want you to love those who want to kill us. I want you to love them without limit and without end. I want you to make peace with them."

My message will never change. All I have to give is love, and this was one of our tests of love.

We could have left and gone to America to escape all the craziness. We could have gone to the international press and fought our case, but we kept hearing the Lord call us to love and forgive. To encourage me in this difficult time, Rolland printed Bible verses and pasted them on the wall. I thought my life was over for a while. I had not eaten or slept for days. Our hearts were broken. Our spirits were crushed. We needed a miracle from heaven.

To answer our prayers, God came and did the first multiplication miracle that I had ever seen. He brought a lady from Texas to our office. She had made chili and rice in a pot to feed our family of four.

I opened the door with nearly a hundred children in the yard, and she got a bit of a shock. She was stunned when she saw the size of our family. She cried, "I have the chili for a family of four." I told her I had a big family and not to worry.

So I looked at her and asked her simply to pray. This upset her; she wanted to go home and cook more. So, she halfheartedly prayed, "God bless it, amen!"

I am not sure I felt like a peacemaker just then, but I still knew I was a daughter. I think I was too hungry and tired to know what I was doing, so I told the children to sit on the grass mats and get ready for dinner by worshipping Jesus. At the time I did not know that God multiplied plastic plates too, but we had enough in our office. One of our Mozambican daughters, Rabia, and our co-worker friend, Maria, helped serve everyone from a little pot of rice, cornmeal, and chili. I asked them to give the children big helpings because they were very hungry.

In the end, every child ate! For the first time in my life, I saw that there is always enough. God indeed provided for His children in our time of great need.

Chapter 17

LOVE—GOD'S PRESERVATIVE

Do not withhold Your tender mercies from
me, O LORD; let Your lovingkindness and
Your truth continually preserve me.

—PSALM 40:11, NKJV

THERE WILL BE a time when each of us will stand before Jesus Christ and He will open a door called "reality past." There we shall gaze into the days of our earthly existence. Jesus will not only commend our lives in a general way, but He will also point to specific things we did. Rejoicing together with us, He will say, "Well done!" Perhaps there was a special act of kindness that turned a bitter person back toward God, or perhaps you overcame your fears and led a person to Christ whom God then used to win thousands.*

In the Latin translation of the Bible, the phrase "well done" is rendered "Bravo!" How would you like Jesus to say that to you? Imagine Him with His arm around your shoulder, saying, "Bravo! You were just an average person,

---

* Francis Frangipane, *The Shelter of the Most High* (Lake Mary, FL: Charisma House, 2008), 145–147.

but you trusted Me; you learned to love without fear. Look how many hearts we touched together!" To be so pleasing to Christ that He rejoices over the life we give Him should be our highest goal.

Yet it is here, in a world filled with devils, devil-possessed people, and conflicts of all sorts, that we must find the life of Christ. In fact, Jesus warned about the Great Tribulation; one meaning of the word *tribulation* is "pressure." Even today are not stress and pressure increasing on people? In spite of these tensions God has called us to love extravagantly. If we do not counteract the stress of this age with love, we will crumble beneath the weight of offenses.

Have you ever seen a supermarket shopping cart full of bent food cans? Most have lost their labels. You can buy a half dozen for a dollar or two. Often what has happened is that the atmospheric pressure outside the can was greater than the pressure inside and the can collapsed. It could not withstand the pressure.

Similarly we must have an aggressive force pushing from the inside out that is equal to the pressures trying to crumble us from the outside. We need the pressure of God's love pouring out through us, neutralizing the pressures of hatred and bitterness in the world.

Love is God's preservative. It surrounds our souls with a power greater than the power of the devil and the world around us. It keeps us balanced. It insulates us against the hostility that exists in our world. Love *is* the shelter of the Most High; it is the substance of God's stronghold.

Chapter 18

GOD IS NOT MAD AT YOU; HE'S MADLY IN LOVE WITH YOU

How great is the love the Father has lavished on us, that we sould be called children of God!

—1 John 3:1, niv

G OD WANTS YOU to know that no matter what you have done, He will never leave you or forsake you. That is God's heart for you and me. He is waiting. He is watching. He will accept you back in. He isn't mad at you. Nope! He is mad about you! You are the apple of His eye. He created you so He could have a relationship with you. He is a good Dad. I want to spend the rest of this chapter sharing five ways God proves He isn't mad at you.*

1. God never stops loving you.

No matter where you are from, where you have been, or the mistakes you have made, God loves you. There is nothing that can get in the way of that. Romans 8:38–39

---

* Pat Schatzline, *Why Is God So Mad at Me?* (Lake Mary, FL: Charisma House, 2013), 173–177.

says, "For I am convinced that neither death nor life, neither angels nor demons, neither the present nor the future, nor any powers, neither height nor depth, nor anything else in all creation, will be able to separate us from the love of God that is in Christ Jesus our Lord" (NIV). Nothing means *nothing*. In 1 John 4:8 the apostle John makes a very profound statement: "Whoever does not love does not know God, because *God is love*" (NIV, emphasis added). In fact, the chapter goes on to say, "We love because he first loved us" (v. 19, NIV). God is love, and His love for us has no limit.

2. God created you for a purpose.

When Paul was confronting the philosophers of the day at a place called Mars Hill, he painted a vivid picture for them of who God is. He said: "The God who made the world and everything in it, this Master of sky and land, doesn't live in custom-made shrines or need the human race to run errands for him, as if he couldn't take care of himself. He makes the creatures; the creatures don't make him. Starting from scratch, he made the entire human race and made the earth hospitable, with plenty of time and space for living so we could seek after God, and not just grope around in the dark but actually find him. He doesn't play hide-and-seek with us. He's not remote; he's near. We live and move in him, can't get away from him! One of your poets said it well: 'We're the God-created.' Well, if we are the God-created, it doesn't make a lot of sense to think we could hire a sculptor to chisel a god out of stone for us, does it?" (Acts 17:24–29, THE MESSAGE).

You are "the God-created," and He made you with a

destiny and purpose in mind. He didn't create you to sit and do nothing. He chose you to walk in power, freedom, and victory. He has a plan for you and your family. God reveals His purpose through your gifts and talents. What brings you joy? That may be the very thing God has called you to do. I challenge you to use your abilities to bring God glory. That doesn't mean you have to preach, sing, or do drama; it just means you make yourself available to be used by Him. God doesn't use the qualified; He qualifies the called.

3. God wants to give you an abundant life!

The devil would love to destroy you, but God wants you to have an abundant life that is filled with His power and provision! John 10:10 says, "The thief comes only to steal and kill and destroy; I have come that they may have life, and have it to the full" (NIV). There is not a single need you have that God doesn't want to fulfill. Psalm 145:15–16 confirms this when it says, "The eyes of all look to you, and you give them their food at the proper time. You open your hand and satisfy the desires of every living thing" (NIV).

God will do more for you than you can imagine. Ephesians 3:20 says God "is able to do immeasurably more than all we ask or imagine, according to his power that is at work within us" (NIV). In Philippians 4:19 God promises that He will take care of every one of your needs "according to his glorious riches in Christ Jesus" (NIV). As my dear friend Dave Martin always says, "The rest of your life is the best of your life!" Believe that God will provide all that you need and get ready to live at another level.

4. God gave His Son as a sacrifice to cover all your sins!

God loved you and me so much that He sent His Son to die for us (John 3:16). We had no way to God, but Jesus made it possible, and this pleased God. Ephesians 1:4–5 says, "Because of his love God had already decided that through Jesus Christ he would make us his children—this was his pleasure and purpose" (GNT). Look at how the prophet Isaiah so beautifully described what Jesus endured for you and me.

> The servant grew up before God—a scrawny seedling, a scrubby plant in a parched field. There was nothing attractive about him, nothing to cause us to take a second look. He was looked down on and passed over, a man who suffered, who knew pain firsthand. One look at him and people turned away. We looked down on him, thought he was scum. But the fact is, it was our pains he carried—our disfigurements, all the things wrong with us. We thought he brought it on himself, that God was punishing him for his own failures. But it was our sins that did that to him, that ripped and tore and crushed him—our sins! He took the punishment, and that made us whole. Through his bruises we get healed. We're all like sheep who've wandered off and gotten lost. We've all done our own thing, gone our own way. And GOD has piled all our sins, everything we've done wrong, on him, on him.
>
> —ISAIAH 53:2–3, THE MESSAGE

Jesus took our pain and sorrow, and He became the sacrifice that brings us freedom. I love the way Romans 8:3–4 explains what Jesus did. It says, "God went for the jugular when he sent his own Son. He didn't deal with the problem as something remote and unimportant. In his Son, Jesus, he personally took on the human condition, entered the disordered mess of struggling humanity in order to set it right once and for all. The law code, weakened as it always was by fractured human nature, could never have done that" (THE MESSAGE). The guy in me loves the first part of that verse—"God went for the jugular"! That phrase perfectly describes the bold and intense moment when Jesus stepped into our humanity and broke the law to rescue you and me! And He did that because He loved us.

5. God has prepared a place in heaven for you.

This earth is not our home! God prepared something else for us. He prepared a place where we will be able to spend eternity with our loving and faithful Father! Jesus is getting my house ready for me right now. Look at this promise in John 14:1–4: "Don't let this throw you. You trust God, don't you? Trust me. There is plenty of room for you in my Father's home. If that weren't so, would I have told you that I'm on my way to get a room ready for you? And if I'm on my way to get your room ready, I'll come back and get you so you can live where I live. And you already know the road I'm taking" (THE MESSAGE). If you have ever doubted the existence of heaven, just read the entire Book of Revelation.

There will come a time when God will call us home to be with Him. First Thessalonians 4:15–17 says, "The Master himself will give the command. Archangel thunder! God's trumpet blast! He'll come down from heaven and the dead in Christ will rise—they'll go first. Then the rest of us who are still alive at the time will be caught up with them into the clouds to meet the Master. Oh, we'll be walking on air! And then there will be one huge family reunion with the Master. So reassure one another with these words" (THE MESSAGE).

This is our promise! That is why the apostle Paul said, "Hey, make sure you tell each other about this. Encourage each other! We are biding our time for a greater place that awaits us." The writer of Hebrews wrote of those who had stood the test of faith. None of them received all that God had promised them, yet they died still believing. The Bible says they were able to have this kind of faith because they knew they were transients in this world. "People who live this way make it plain that they are looking for their true home. If they were homesick for the old country, they could have gone back any time they wanted. But they were after a far better country than that—heaven country. You can see why God is so proud of them, and has a City waiting for them" (Heb. 11:13–16, THE MESSAGE).

God isn't mad at you. He wants to spend eternity with you. Would you want to live forever with someone you were mad at? God doesn't either. He wants you to be with Him because He delights in you.

Chapter 19

LETTING GOD LOVE US

Yes, I have loved you with an everlasting love;
therefore with lovingkindness I have drawn you.
—Jeremiah 31:3, NKJV

It is my opinion, having been a pastor for many years, that the hardest thing in the world to believe is that God really loves us. It is harder to believe that than to believe that there is a God or that Jesus died on the cross or even that He rose from the dead. It's not too difficult to believe that God will take care of you or that "in all things God works for the good of those who love him" (Rom. 8:28, NIV), though we may not believe that they are for our good at the time.[*]

But there is an even more dazzling truth, and that is that God loves you as much as He loves Jesus. Have you any idea how much God loves Jesus? Have you any idea how God feels about His one and only Son? The voice that came from heaven at Jesus's baptism said, "You are my Son, whom I love; with you I am well pleased" (Mark 1:11, NIV).

---

[*] R. T. Kendall, *When God Shows Up* (Lake Mary, FL: Charisma House, 2008), 129–133, 136–137, 139–140.

The voice that came at the Mount of Transfiguration said, "This is my Son, whom I love. Listen to him!" (Mark 9:7, NIV).

In John 17:23 Jesus actually prayed that we would see that God loves us as much as He Himself is loved: "May they be brought to complete unity to let the world know that you sent me and have loved them even as you have loved me" (NIV).

God chose us before we were born (Rom. 9:11), yet He knows what we are like. Jesus could say to Nathanael, "I saw you while you were still under the fig tree before Philip called you" (John 1:48, NIV). As Gerald Coates has put it, God does not get disillusioned with us, because He never had any illusions in the first place!

I don't understand the rationale behind God's choosing me; I only know that it is not based on works (2 Tim. 1:9). Those God loves He has already chosen, and when we let God love us, we dignify His choice of us, however unworthy we feel. He wants us to know how deeply He cares and to affirm this.

First John 4:16 is a verse you could read a thousand times and yet not fully grasp. The King James Version says, "And we have known and believed the love that God hath to us." It's easy to read that and not take it in. The NIV makes it a little clearer: "And so we know and rely on the love God has for us." I wonder if you have reached the stage where you just rely on God's love for you.

You cannot rely very long on your love for God. But can you rely on His love for you? He wants you to. Just think how much it would thrill Him if you really believed He loves you.

I find it difficult to believe God loves me. For this reason, a few years ago I began doing something at the beginning of the day when I spent time alone with the Lord to pray. I still do it now. I refer to two Scripture references: Hebrews 4:16 and 1 John 4:16. The first says, "Let us then approach the throne of grace with confidence, so that we may receive mercy and find grace to help us in our time of need" (NIV). The second, 1 John 4:16, is the verse quoted earlier: "And so we know and rely on the love God has for us" (NIV). So every day I'm aware that I'm asking for mercy, but I'm believing in His love. I have come to see that it really is true: God loves me. God loves you. God really does love us.

When I have to battle unbelief, I refuse to accept any other option but to rely on His love. I believe it. Any other thought will come from the devil, who doesn't want us to believe that God loves us, who will accuse us and call to our attention every sin we have committed in the past to cast us down. The devil doesn't want you to believe that God loves you, but God loves you very much, and He loves you just as you are.

We have all had bad moments when we feel unworthy. I want to tell you what I do at my lowest moments. If I'm ever at rock bottom (and I wouldn't want you to know how often that is), I remember I know it's true that He died for us all. I hang on to those verses that say He died for everybody.

My own experience is that God has a way of drawing near to me when I feel at my most unlovable. All of a sudden I sense His presence, and I'm amazed. I think, "Lord, You can't do this. Of all the times for You to manifest Your love to me!" God loves to do that. When you are feeling at your most unworthy and least deserving—I don't know why—He'll just love you.

You'll feel the way the disciples felt on the evening of that first day of the week after Jesus's crucifixion, as they hid themselves away, terrified of reprisals from the Jewish authorities. They had denied Jesus, fleeing from Him when He most needed them. Now He's risen from the dead, and He walks through a locked door, saying, "Peace be with you!" (John 20:19, NIV). Jesus could even say to Simon Peter, "You will disown me three times! Do not let your hearts be troubled. Trust in God; trust also in me" (John 13:38–14:1, NIV).

You see, God just keeps on loving us. Loving us with an everlasting love.

Chapter 20

FEELING LOVED

How precious also are Your thoughts to me, O God!
How great is the sum of them! If I should count them,
they would be more in number than the sand.

—PSALM 139:17–18, NKJV

GOD WANTS YOU to go beyond merely knowing that He loves you. He wants you to move past simply believing and affirming by faith that He loves you. He wants you to taste it! He wants you to get out of your car, take off your shoes and socks, jump in, and get wet! He wants you to feel the joy of being loved. He wants you to receive His love personally and powerfully in a way that is life changing. He wants you to wade in it, swim in it, and to be refreshed by drinking of it to your heart's delight and fill.*

I'm overwhelmed to hear that God loves me. Sermons on God's love are uplifting and edifying. Writing a book about it has contributed immensely to my understanding and appreciation of the vast dimensions of God's commitment to my soul's ultimate and lasting welfare.

---

* Sam Storms, *The Singing God* (Lake Mary, FL: Passio, 2013), 136–138, 146–147.

But that's not enough. It's not that I'm a demanding person by nature. I don't think my attitude is born of sinful discontent. I honestly believe that the Holy Spirit is responsible for my craving to feel God's love. I yearn in the depths of my heart to experience in a passionate and powerful way the reality and presence of God's affection.

I know that I run the risk of being accused of anti-intellectualism or perhaps emotional fanaticism. I am careful to deal honestly with the text of Scripture. I address your mind and challenge you to think reasonably and rationally about what God's love for us means and implies.

But there's more to it than that. We are more than our minds. There is more to being loved by the Creator of the universe than seeing it in the pages of the Bible or reading about it in the pages of this book. True love, genuine love is experienced love. Love that isn't felt may certainly be real, but it is just as certainly incomplete.

I want us to go beyond God's love as a mere spectacle. There is a dimension to being loved by God that transcends apprehending it intellectually. It is more than an objective fact, more than something "out there" to admire and observe. It is also a subjective experience, something "in here" to feel and enjoy.

My fear is that too many Christians experience God's love in the same way they do a great painting. If you have ever attended the exhibit of a famous art collection, you know that extensive measures are employed to keep the viewing public at more than arm's length from the various works on display. Often as with the *Mona Lisa* (in the Louvre in Paris France), the painting is kept behind a glass enclosure. Security guards are positioned so that no one can get too close. Strategically placed signs warn of the consequences to be exacted from those who dare to cross cordoned-off areas.

The result is that the viewing public is reduced to precisely that: viewing. They are mere spectators. I suppose in an art gallery that houses priceless masterpieces this is the only reasonable policy. But it won't do when it comes to God's love for His children. God's love is not to be viewed from afar but deeply and intimately embraced. Come close, touch, smell, feel, and enjoy the warmth of relationship with the author of this heavenly affection.

God built you with the capacity to feel and experience spiritual ecstasy so that He might be glorified in your enjoyment of Him! Emotions are to be enjoyed. Feelings are for fun.

Don't take my word for it. Listen to what God commends and commands relative to your emotional life.

> You have made known to me that path of life; you
> will fill me with joy in your presence, with eternal
> pleasures at your right hand.
> —Psalm 16:11, niv

> Delight yourself in the Lord and he will give you
> the desires of your heart.
> —Psalm 37:4, niv

> They feast on the abundance of your house; you
> give them drink from your river of delights.
> —Psalm 36:8, niv

Elsewhere the psalmist speaks about a passionate yearning for God that can only be compared to the relentless search for water by a thirsty deer (Ps. 42:1–2; 63:1) and to find to Him "exceeding joy" (Ps. 43:4, NAS).

After Jesus revealed His identity to the two disciples on the Emmaus road, they exclaimed, "Were not our hearts burning within us while he talked with us on the road and opened the Scriptures to us?" (Luke 24:32, NIV). Their minds were enlightened to understand and they felt the effects of it in their whole being. This is what I call a case of "spiritual heartburn!" But whatever you do, don't take a Tums! Enjoy the heat!

What did they feel? Perhaps they experienced a rapid heartbeat, chills down their spines, maybe even bodily weakness that made it difficult to stand erect. Their breathing may have quickened as they began to feel lightheaded. Perhaps they trembled and wept and rejoiced.

Does your heart "burn" within when you think of God singing in love over you? It should. It's OK. God wants it to. Deep down inside I suspect you want it to also. God longs for you to feel deep and lasting satisfaction in Him. That is the principal way He is glorified in you. So enjoy Him. Receive His love for you and revel in it. Let His affection for your soul lift you to unknown heights of spiritual ecstasy. Honor Him by being happy in Him.

Get on your knees and drink the cool, refreshing waters of God's love! It tastes so good! It quenches the thirsty soul and renews the sagging spirit! And best of all, it glorifies God.

PART 5

HOPE IN DREAMS

Chapter 21

NEVER DOUBT YOUR DREAM

For what if some did not believe? shall their unbelief
make the faith of God without effect? God forbid: yea,
let God be true, but every man a liar; as it is written.

—Romans 3:3–4, kjv

WHAT DO YOU do when your world does not look like
your word; when you have a word from God over
your life, but your present situation doesn't look like the
dream God gave you?*

Never doubt the vision God gave you, because I know
that God will back up the dreams and visions that He puts
into people's hearts. You should never doubt your vision
because you should never doubt your God.

It doesn't matter how long it takes to see your dream
come to fruition. It doesn't matter if your vision is a big one
or a little one. If God is in it, it's in the bag. If He inspired
it in the first place, He will see it through to completion.

---

* Jentezen Franklin, *Believe That You Can* (Lake Mary, FL: Charisma
House, 2008), 165, 176–178.

So What If They Don't Believe?

So what if "they" say it won't happen? So what if people laugh and mock the dream that God has given you? They mocked Noah when he started building an ark in the middle of a drought, but he's the one who had the last laugh.

The simple fact is this: your God is a rock. He will not fail. He won't even miss a step.

Other people don't have to believe in you in order for your dream to come true. It's your dream. God gave it to *you*, not to them. They don't have to believe. It's not up to them at all. They're not the ones who are carrying that dream on the inside of them like you are. You're the dream carrier, and what God plans to do does not depend upon the affirmation of the people around you. Paul said, "For what if some did not believe? shall their unbelief make the faith of God without effect? God forbid: yea, let God be true, but every man a liar; as it is written" (Rom. 3:3–4, KJV).

Paul knew what he was talking about, because when he got knocked off his horse on the road to Damascus, the church people found it very hard to believe that Paul (Saul of Tarsus, who had persecuted the church mercilessly) had even become a Christian, let alone to trust that God had a plan for using him. Naturally they thought he was faking it. (See Acts 9:26.)

But it didn't matter to Paul. Paul just kept hanging on to his vision and to the Lord, who had given it to him. He faced all the opposition calmly. He probably expected it. He models for us what I call "stand-alone" faith, the kind of faith that keeps moving forward, even in the face of disbelief and antagonism.

When all the voices around you tell you that you cannot accomplish the dream that God has given you and that it will not happen, God wants to give you that kind of faith. He wants you to be able to say, "So what if they don't believe? They can't cancel out what God has put into me."

When you have a real dream, "they" can throw you into a pit and your dream will still happen! Remember Joseph? When you have a real dream, "they" can lie about you and defame your good name. They can accuse you of crimes you didn't commit. That's what happened when Potiphar's wife accused Joseph of raping her. But even if they throw you into prison, your dream isn't locked up. Even if "they" overlook you for promotion and ignore you and act like they never heard of you, God will see your dream through. So what if they don't believe?

If you have a real dream from God, it won't die in the face of opposition. So what if nobody has ever done your dream before? So what if even talented and qualified people have tried and failed to do what you believe God has anointed you to do? So what if the doctor has never seen anybody recover from what you have? So what? Let God be true and every man a liar!

Chapter 22

PUT AWAY YOUR MEASURING STICK

*I lifted up mine eyes again, and looked, and behold
a man with a measuring line in his hand....And,
behold, the angel that talked with me went forth,
and another angel went out to meet him.*

—ZECHARIAH 2:1, 3, KJV

WHEREVER YOU FIND yourself in the process, don't put
limits on what God can do! He is infinite, and so are
the possibilities for the dreams that He gives people. The
trouble is, we have a very strong tendency to put limits on
Him, especially when it comes to our dreams and visions
for our lives. We think we are the final authority on our
lives and that we know what's best and what's realistic.*

Be careful that you don't end up trying to stand against
God just because you think you know what you're doing.
God Himself doesn't want you to keep measuring yourself or your circumstances against your idea of reality. How
do I know that? Because He put what He thinks about
"measuring" in the Bible: "I lifted up mine eyes again, and

---

* Jentezen Franklin, *Believe That You Can* (Lake Mary, FL: Charisma
House, 2008), 209–213, 217.

looked, and behold a man with a measuring line in his hand.... And, behold, the angel that talked with me went forth, and another angel went out to meet him" (Zech. 2:1, 3, KJV).

See the picture in your mind. There was a young man who took a measuring line because he was going to try to measure what God was doing in the city of Jerusalem. *God was disturbed by that.* He was disturbed enough to dispatch an angel from heaven on the spot to stop him. And when the angel said to the young man, "Son, what are you doing?" and the man said that he was going to measure the width, breadth, and height of Jerusalem to see what God was doing in the earth, the angel said back to him, "Put your measuring line away, son, because anything that God is involved in is *unmeasurable.*"

God didn't want anybody to put limits on what He could or would do. God knew that as soon as people starting measuring the city, they would define the boundaries. They would tend to set boundaries, and they would box God in. Their measurements would make a statement about what they felt God is capable of.

This idea of measuring lines has a lot of application, because instead of believing that we can accomplish what God gives us to do (even if it seems impossible), we put limits on everything. In theory we may believe that God can accomplish the impossible, but in practice we draw boundaries.

God says, "I'm going to use you," and your first response is, "But I come from the bad side of town. I don't have any education. My daddy left my family when I was a kid. I have so many handicaps..."

Don't you think your response should be more like Mary's response? The angel told her that she would become pregnant even though she was a virgin and that she would bear the Son of God. She was startled, but she didn't object to the word. Her response was, "How shall this be?...Behold the handmaid of the Lord; be it unto me according to thy word" (Luke 1:34, 38, KJV). No ifs, ands, or buts. She didn't put any limits on her unlimited God.

Unlimited Supply

Some of you have looked at your bills recently. Maybe you just did it again last night. And then you looked at your paycheck, and it's not enough to pay them. Out came your old measuring tape, and you said, as the disciples said before the Lord multiplied a few loaves and fish to feed five thousand-plus people, "What are they among so many?" (John 6:9, KJV). One of the disciples even said, "If we had two hundred pennies worth of bread, it would only be enough for a few of them, and we don't even have that much." (See Mark 6:37; John 6:7.) Your version is, "See, what is so little income with so many bills? Even if I had two jobs, it wouldn't be enough."

That's a tape-measure mentality in action. Over against our limited version of the possibilities, we have God. God has a "maximum mentality." You need to stop applying your minimum mentality with your maximum God. You need to stop measuring your earning capacity by what you earned last year or by your previous achievements in the working world. That just puts a cap on what God can do.

He is a God of increase. He is a God of abundance. With Him, if we will only give Him what we have and trust Him with it, and begin to obey Him when He tells us what to do, we will start to see increase. Get rid of that measuring tape. Sell it on eBay or something. Get it out of your house!

Once you've had increase in your life, you will be able to recognize that it wasn't your brilliance that did it. It was God's doing. He could have left you back in your field as a sower. All your life you could have kept sowing and resowing the seed. But He gave the increase, and now you can see the whole picture.

Let your dream live, and let it flow! You can flow with it. God wants you to grab hold of your dream so that at the end of your life on Earth you can say with the apostle Paul, "I was not disobedient unto the heavenly vision" (Acts 26:19, KJV). Put away your measuring line, and let God take you to meet your destiny.

Believe that you can! "For with God nothing shall be impossible" (Luke 1:37, KJV)!

Chapter 23

DREAMS FULFILLED

*For the vision is yet for an appointed time and
it hastens to the end [fulfillment]; it will not
deceive or disappoint. Though it tarry, wait [ear-
nestly] for it, because it will surely come.*

—HABAKKUK 2:3, AMP

LIKE DEFEATED ENEMIES, frightened, cowed, and
hoping only to preserve their lives, they bowed before
him. Joseph's dreams had come true. At last, at long last,
far away from where he had dreamed it, in a strange and
foreign land that was now home to him, his dreams had
come true. (See Genesis 43–50.)*

Egypt—he could never have predicted that. On that
fateful night so long ago, in his childlike dreams he had
seen this moment, this day of dominion with his family
bowing to him as to an oriental potentate. Joseph remembered those dreams as though he had dreamed them last
night. Those dreams had never faded, never been forgotten,
were always there just under the surface of the soul, holding

---

* Mark Rutland, *Dream* (Lake Mary, FL: Charisma House, 2003), 89–91.

him even as he held on to them. From dream to fulfillment, from his father's tents to Pharaoh's palace, his dreams had carried him into Egypt and to his destiny.

As Joseph's family knelt before him in abject need, broken, repentant, and fully submitted, the bizarre course of his life flashed before him like a lightning bolt. How could that which had been lived out over long years of pain and humiliation now pass through his mind in a second? Was this also a dream? Would he awaken from this moment to find himself in the predawn back in his father's tents?

No, this was no dream. This was real, as real as the pit, the prison, and the palace through which he had passed as a slave, then as a convict, and here, at last, as the king's regent in the land of the mighty pharaohs. This was really his family before him on a real floor, before his very real throne.

How strange, how curious, how very like God that his passage from childhood dream to manhood's realization should have been through such remarkable twists and turns. The more Joseph understood of both God and dreams, the more convinced he became that a dream is one of God's greatest gifts. Now he also knew, had learned the hard way, that a dream dreamed in Canaan may look not at all as you might expect when it finally finds fulfillment in Egypt. Dreams do not explain the future; the future will finally explain the dream.

So this was what it all meant. Their sheaves were, at last, bowing to his. The sun, moon, and stars—the celestial family that had rejected and betrayed him now knelt at his feet, pleading for their lives. The dream, now coming true before his very eyes, gave him at once some sense of closure and a touch of the same old uncertainty of a dream as yet unfilled.

"Stay here," he told them. "You shall want for nothing, not even land. You are herdsmen, and Pharaoh has allowed me to grant you the province of Goshen, Egypt's richest grazing lands. Go down there and live. Take all your herds and flocks and your little ones, and may all your dreams come true."

"We have nothing to offer in return," Reuben said.

"I want only this, a promise. Tell your children, tell them to tell theirs, forever, from generation to generation. When your descendants return to The Land, they must take my bones. I forgive everything. The dream is fulfilled. God used even your wicked intentions to bring about His divine purpose. You were brought here to Egypt by the power of a dream. So was I. Why, I do not know.

"What I do know is that a dream gives way to dream. Here by a dream; home by a dream. Do not leave my bones in Egypt. That I will not forgive. Let this be remembered in Egypt, and let it never be forgotten in the land of Goshen. Someday the children of Israel will go home. When they do, let them carry up with them the mummy of Joseph."

"How strange," he thought, when they were ushered out of his presence. How strange indeed. In the land of Israel he dreamed of Egypt, but in Egypt he dreamed of The Land.

Chapter 24

WITH A DREAM
YOU CAN MAKE IT

*Though my father and mother for-
sake me, the LORD will receive me.*

—PSALM 27:10, NIV

ONE NIGHT A young man attended the youth meeting
at the Dream Center and responded to the invitation
to come forward to accept Jesus as his personal Savior. That
night Manuel gave his heart to Jesus and was saved.*

As Manuel prayed with the youth workers at the altar,
the discouraging details of his life began to emerge. His
dad was a drug user who had contracted AIDS. Manuel's
mother, unable to deal with the abuse of drugs any longer,
had left, leaving Manuel, a fifteen-year-old boy, alone with
his father. Manuel was ashamed of his father, and their
relationship had broken down—each closing himself off in
his own private despair.

But after Manuel accepted Jesus as his Savior, he was

---

* Tommy Barnett, *Dream Again* (Lake Mary, FL: Charisma House, 1998),
187–189.

determined to be restored in his relationship with his father. He brought his father to church, where his father also accepted Jesus as his Savior. But the disease of AIDS continued to ravage his father's body.

"How can there be a God, if He would destroy my dad?" Manuel cried out to the youth pastor. "He's all I've got. If he dies, I'll be without parents—without anybody in the whole world!"

The youth pastor prayed diligently with Manuel for several hours—to no avail. Manuel could not find peace. Finally, about 10:00 p.m. the youth pastor sent someone to knock gently on Jim Bakker's door. "Can you help?" the worker asked. "We have been praying with Manuel, but nothing seems to help him."

Jim immediately dressed and went to talk with Manuel. For the next hour and a half he tried to give Manuel every promise he could find in God's Word. But none of it seemed to bring any hope to Manuel.

In desperation Jim felt led to share his own story with Manuel. "At one time I had three thousand people working for me," Jim said. "I had beautiful homes, cars, even a seventy-foot boat. But overnight I lost everything."

Then, as Jim's voice began to break, he continued. "From the middle of prison I watched on television as my house burned to the ground. Then I found out that my wife—the one I loved most—was divorcing me to marry the man I had thought was my best friend." He looked right into Manuel's eyes and repeated, "Manuel, I lost the one I loved the most. But today I love Jesus more than ever. He *never* left me, *never* forsook me. Jesus promised in His Word that

He would *never, never* leave me or forsake me—and He hasn't."

Manuel listened carefully to Jim's story. He looked right at Jim and said, "Mr. Bakker, if you could make it, then I know I will be able to make it too."

At that moment one of the greatest healings in Jim Bakker's life took place. All the pain of his prison years faded away as he looked in that boy's face. He realized that God was turning the pain of his own experience into positive gain—God was using *him* to help others!

A few days later Manuel's father died, and Matthew preached His funeral. The people at the Dream Center took up a collection and bought Manuel one of the required school uniforms so he could attend school at the Dream Center.

Manuel's newfound faith in God saw him through. He thanked God for his salvation and for his father's salvation. He moved into the Dream Center. Everyone at the center— staff and people in the various programs—"adopted" Manuel as one of their own. Because Jim Bakker learned to dream again—Manuel did too!

Chapter 25

THERE'S A MIRACLE
DREAM IN YOUR HOUSE

*What shall I do for you? Tell me, what
do you have in the house?*

—2 KINGS 4:2, NKJV

JUST AS GOD gave us the Holy Spirit, He gives us all the
resources and abilities we need to fulfill our dreams. God
never gives us dreams without giving us the tools to make
them possible. Not only is there a dream in your house, but
there is also a miracle in your house to fulfill it.*

What does it mean to have "a miracle in your house"?
Second Kings 4:2–7 shows us in the circumstance of a
widow whose creditor was about to take two children away
from her because she had run out of money.

> A certain woman of the wives of the sons of the
> prophets cried out to Elisha, saying, "Your ser-
> vant my husband is dead, and you know that

---

* Tommy Barnett, *Reaching Your Dreams* (Lake Mary, FL: Charisma
House, 2005), 159–161, 165–166.

your servant feared the LORD. And the creditor is coming to take my two sons to be his slaves."

So Elisha said to her, "What shall I do for you? Tell me, what do you have in the house?" And she said, "Your maidservant has nothing in the house but a jar of oil."

Then he said, "Go borrow vessels from everywhere from all your neighbors—empty vessels; do not gather just a few. And when you have come in, you shall shut the door behind you and your sons; then pour it into all those vessels, and set aside the full ones."

So she went from him and shut the door behind her and her sons, who brought the vessels to her; and she poured it out. Now it came to pass, when the vessels were full, that she said to her son, "Bring me another vessel."

And he said to her, "There is not another vessel." So the oil ceased. Then she came and told the man of God. And he said, "Go, sell the oil and pay your dept; and you and your sons live on the rest."

—NKJV

This biblical example lays out the pattern of finding the miracle for your dream in your house.

First, we must find out what is in the house—what resources we have, what talents and experience, what contacts. Like that widow, we too often get caught up in what we don't have and lose sight of the provision God has already made available. The beginning of a miracle was literally in her kitchen, but she didn't see it because it was too small.

Some people think they have to rely on outside money, outside talent, or outside manpower to reach their dreams. They think the resources for accomplishing their dreams are in other people's hands, so they spend a lot of time trying to convince others to support them. But the opposite is really true. Each person reading this book has been given the resources, or access to the resources to carry out his or her dream. Perhaps you think you have nothing— but that is simply never true. Every person has a mind, physical strength, experience, and knowledge. Because you are a Christian, the Holy Spirit lives in your "house." Christ lives in your house, in all His omnipotence and omnipresence. God Himself indwells you; His resources are yours. Far from having nothing, you have everything. Second Peter 1:3 says: "As His divine power has given to us all things that pertain to life and godliness, through the knowledge of Him who called us by glory and virtue" (NKJV).

You have everything you need. So what is in your house? Do an inventory assessment. List your talents, gifts, skills, and firsthand experience. List your bank account balance, investments, and property. List your friends, colleagues, contacts, and coworkers. Perhaps you are overlooking a small miracle that could easily grow into huge provision. Maybe you have an idea for a product, service, or business you consider interesting but probably insignificant. Did you know that every great corporation, every great work of God, every great invention began as a seemingly insignificant idea? Don't despise those small ideas. They may be the very thoughts God gave you! His intentions often come in the form of ideas that occur to you like sparks of creativity. I would venture to say that God has already shared ideas with you that could change your life and the world.

When God works in your dream, He gives three things: a plan, a promise, and power. God gave Abraham the plan: "I want you to be father of a great nation." Then came a promise: "I'll multiply your offspring like the sand on the seashore." Last came the power to conceive at an old age. God gave Moses a plan, "Free My people"; a promise, "I'll be with you wherever you go"; and the power to do miracles before Pharaoh. Jesus gave the disciples a plan, "Go and make disciples of all nations"; a promise, "I'll be with you even to the end of the age"; and the power (Acts 2).

Don't you see the sequence? The plan and promise always come before the power. The problem for many of us is that we want power first. One Christian prayed for years, "Give me more power, more power!" Finally God said, "With plans no bigger than yours, you don't need more power." Many people don't need the power of God to fulfill their plans. It's not enough to believe in miracles; you have to depend on them.

What you ask or think can put a limit on God's power in your life. I would encourage you, don't limit God's ability to provide. Believe for the plan and promise of your dream, for the Lord said to the widow through the prophet, "Go borrow. Get as many vessels as you can." Even when things look small, plan big. Remember, the dream must be so big that if it becomes reality, everybody will know it had to be God.

Fill your house with expectancy. Conduct an inventory of what you have and whom you know. Then take action and start pouring! The best promise of the widow's story is that the miraculous supply of oil kept flowing until every vessel was filled. There is no shortage with God! He has put the seeds of a miracle in your house that will bring your dream into reality. Your "house" may be your church, your business, your school, your home, your workplace, and your day-care center. All the creativity, finances, and resources for your dream are in that house in one form or another.

Dream big: then discover the miracle in your house!

PART 6

HOPE IN
THE PRESENCE OF GOD

Chapter 26

THE VALUE OF WORSHIP

*Exalt ye the LORD our God, and wor-
ship at his footstool; for he is holy.*

—PSALM 99:5, KJV

THE PROPHET HABAKKUK was lamenting the condition of his people, for he looked around and saw violence, law-breaking, and injustice everywhere. Surveying these insurmountable problems with his natural eyes, he became discouraged. He knew he needed to hear from God, so he set himself to seek God: "I will stand on my guard post and station myself on the rampart; and I will keep watch to see what He will speak to me, and how I may reply when I am reproved" (Hab. 2:1, NAS). The guard post was the highest point on the wall surrounding the city. It was here, as Habakkuk waited, that God responded to him, giving him a vision and speaking to him personally.*

God's manifest presence changed Habakkuk's perspective, and he took heart that God was going to visit His people once again. He was filled with awe as he declared,

---

* Fuchsia Pickett, *Worship Him* (Lake Mary, FL: Charisma House, 2000), 138–145.

"But the LORD is in His holy temple. Let all the earth be silent before Him" (v. 20, NAS). His questions were answered, his heart encouraged, and his prayer life renewed by this divine visitation. Waiting before God had brought a life-giving response to Habakkuk from God.

When God puts a desire in our hearts for something specific to happen in our lives and ministries, and we do not see it coming to pass, we often get discouraged. And the longer we look at seemingly impossible situations and evaluate them according to our natural reasoning, the more discouraged we become. We need to do as Habakkuk did and get up to a high place alone where we can worship God.

Setting ourselves to seek God not only will change our perspective but also will bring an answer from God. He may simply speak peace to our hearts, or He may whisper a verse of Scripture into our spirits that will strengthen us and encourage our hearts. He may reassure us of the fulfillment of our desire, as He did Habakkuk: "For the vision is yet for the appointed time; it hastens toward the goal, and it will not fail. Though it tarries, wait for it; for it will certainly come, it will not delay" (v. 3, NAS). It is in the place of worship that we will find the godly perspective that will give us rest in the perplexities of life.

God's Throne in Our Midst

The psalmist instructs us to "exalt ye the LORD our God, and worship at his footstool; for he is holy" (Ps. 99:5, KJV). Worshipping God dethrones every usurper that would demand our allegiance, perpetrate unbelief in our hearts, or try to thwart the purposes of God for our lives. Enthroning

God in our hearts deals a deathblow to our self-nature, perhaps the greatest enemy to the will of God.

I encourage you to read a psalm of exaltation every day and meditate on the wonder of who God is. It will assure you of victory over every kind of enemy that wants to dethrone the King of kings in your life. God's presence will be made known in our worship, individually and corporately. And where He is, there is life—eternal life, abundant life—and victory over every kind of "death."

A Weapon in Spiritual Warfare

The psalmist praised and blessed the Lord for giving him power over his enemies: "Blessed be the LORD my strength, which teacheth my hands to war, and my fingers to fight" (Ps. 144:1, KJV). David was involved in fighting armies that wanted to destroy the nation of Israel. As Christians, we understand that we are in spiritual warfare against principalities and powers that want to destroy the body of Christ:

> For we wrestle not against flesh and blood, but against principalities, against powers, against the rulers of the darkness of this world, against spiritual wickedness in high places.
> —EPHESIANS 6:12, KJV

The place of worship equips us as warriors against the attacks of the evil one, who wants to destroy the lives of believers as well as those who do not know Christ. Satan hates our worship because he knows the power of it will put him to flight. Praise and worship become a fortress for us against the enemy. Isaiah declared, "Thou shalt call thy walls Salvation, and thy gates Praise" (Isa. 60:18, KJV). We can assume a victorious position through worship, making war in high places.

As we lift our hands in praise and surrender to God, acknowledging His lordship over our lives, we acknowledge the defeat of Satan as well. While we cannot hope to gain victory over an unseen spiritual enemy in our own strength, we can indeed be victorious as we learn to use the spiritual weapons of prayer and praise.

One of Satan's most effective devices is to attack our thoughts, causing us to imagine all kinds of ungodly ideas. How often have you been tormented by feelings of unworthiness, guilt, or just vague uneasiness concerning your relationship with God? Worship becomes a spiritual weapon that pulls down the enemy's strongholds in our imagination, bringing our thoughts into line with the Word of God. The apostle Paul described this warfare:

> For the weapons of our warfare are not carnal, but mighty through God to the pulling down of strong holds; casting down imaginations, and every high thing that exalteth itself against the knowledge of God, and bringing into captivity every thought to the obedience of Christ.
>
> —2 CORINTHIANS 10:4–5, KJV

Worship is a mighty weapon in our arsenal that releases the power of God to deliver us from our enemies and fill our thoughts with the goodness of our God. Our whole lives revolve around the centrality of worship that brings us continually into right relationship with God.

Chapter 27

GOD SAID, "DANCE!"

Then David danced before the L ORD with all his might.
—2 S AMUEL 6:14, NKJV

I REMEMBER AT ONE point, early in my ministry, I was so depressed and discouraged that I just felt like giving up. It seemed nothing was going right, and God had forsaken me. I found myself facing a tough financial crisis trying to birth this ministry, and to top it all off, I had caught wind of something that was said about me that was totally untrue and unfair. There I was—sobbing, lying on the floor, with my nose in the carpet. Of course, I was complaining to God about how terrible things were in my life and how hard I had been working for Him, all for the "prize" of having someone talk about me. I'm sure you have never been there before. Right? Wrong! We have all been there, if we are pressing, pushing, and pursuing.*

As I was lying there feeling sorry for myself, I distinctly heard the Lord say, "Get up and dance!"

I thought to myself, "What was that? Where did that

---

* Judy Jacobs, *Take It by Force!* (Lake Mary, FL: Charisma House, 2005), 206–208.

come from? That wasn't God; that was the devil trying to make fun of me."

Then I heard it again. "Get up and dance!"

I said, "Is that You, Lord?"

He said, "Yes, this is Me; get up and dance."

There is a violent faith that has to come to your shout, your dance, your walk, and your talk if you are going to see victory. Sometimes you will be forced to walk your walk instead of talking your talk.

I thought to myself, "How in the world can I shout, dance, and rejoice in the middle of all of this?" So I said to the Lord, "OK, God; all my life I have tried to obey You, and I'm going to do it now, because I will to obey Your will."

So as I'm lying there, I thought to myself, "I guess I could get up on my knees." And as I did, I thought, "Well I might as well just lift my hands," and as I did that, I remembered thinking, "That feels pretty good." So I opened my mouth and I managed to let out a few "Thank You, Lords" and "I love You, Jesus."

I noticed how uncomfortable I had become on my knees, because normally while I pray, I love to walk. As I raised up on my feet, I noticed that strength came to my whole entire being. I began to walk back and forth a little bit. As I did, the better it felt in that room. Before I knew it, I had both hands raised and my voice was so loud that my neighbor was wondering what in the world was going on. You have never seen anybody dance, jump, leap, and shout the way that I did. Total victory came, and God turned that whole situation around when I chose to obey Him and dance.

God spoke something to me that was so mighty that I will never forget it. He spoke so lovingly to me and said, "You have overestimated the devil in your life, and you have underestimated the power and the anointing of the Holy Spirit in your life. Don't you remember that I will never put more on you than you are able to bear? The devil is a liar, and what he tells you is the exact opposite of what is really happening. If you'll just give Me praise and worship, you will see My glory, and the victory will come."

The joy of violent faith is seeing and having your family saved and walking in total surrender to the Lord with you, not only down here on this earth but also in eternity. This life is short and is only a vapor, but eternity is forever. What greater joy is there to the Father than knowing that His children are saved, free, and delivered from the grip of Satan's power.

Second Peter 3:9 says, "The Lord is not slack concerning his promise, as some men count slackness; but is longsuffering to us-ward, not willing that any should perish, but that all should come to repentance" (kjv).

The heart of the Father God is to see *all* His children free from the bondages of Satan's power.

The joy of violent faith is seeing your body healed, seeing those dreams come to life that once lay dormant and lifeless. The joy of violent faith is trusting and believing that your Father God is in control and that He is Lord, and all things are working together *right now* for your good. You have His promise that He is with you.

So I want to encourage you, and at the same time challenge you, to get up, get moving, get those dancing shoes on, and dance on the devil's head, because He is under your feet. And, by all means, shout for joy; the victory is yours in Jesus's name!

Chapter 28

WAITING FOR HIS PRESENCE

Wait on the LORD; be of good courage, and He shall strengthen your heart; wait, I say, on the LORD!
—PSALM 27:14, NKJV

WE DON'T KNOW how to wait. The Lord calls; He beckons us to come and be with Him, but we don't know how to wait for Him. So often we give up too soon—we get discouraged. But it is worth the wait.*

Instead of waiting, we try to fulfill our desires and longings with substitutes. But what is required of us is simply to wait—sometimes for days. Set aside time for God alone. These are times of remaining quiet, of meditating upon His Word, of sometimes worshipping and always praising Him. The discipline of waiting is something many of us know little about.

When His presence comes into our prayer closets, He often comes with power, love, and passion. His Spirit enters like a mighty, rushing wind—a great big surprise package wrapped with a big bow.

---

* Pat Chen, *Intimacy With the Beloved* (Lake Mary, FL: Charisma House, 2000), 12–14.

When you experience Him in this way, you may cry aloud, "You, Lord, are the joy of my soul's desire! You fill my heart with laughter and song. My heart is filled with love for You, O God. Put back together all the broken pieces of my life. Blow away my insecurities with the breath of Your Spirit. Wash me in Your presence. I want nothing more than to be with You in Your glorious presence."

At other times He may come with utter silence and stillness, and you may not be able to move or speak a word. Such a visitation of God's presence is fearsome.

Our God is truly a God of "suddenlies." He will come upon your waiting heart in an instant. You may also experience long seasons during which you feel nothing and hear nothing as you wait for His presence. It doesn't matter. He is there watching your every move and listening to your every thought. He knows, and He is there with you.

Are you willing to wait silently, expectantly, for Him? Will you pay this price for intimacy with your heavenly Bridegroom? Ask Him to teach you to wait upon Him.

A Garden Locked

Only God can dig this wellspring, and only God can fill it. If you are a believer, deep within your heart is a well of God's Spirit. Much has been placed within you that only God knows about and understands: gifts of the Spirit, anointings, longings, visions, plans, and purposes of God. Others can drink from your wellspring as the life of God flows out of you through your words, actions, and deeds.

Not only can the treasures of God's Spirit deep within you refresh others, but also God Himself desires to be refreshed by your love. This is the communion He desires: "A garden locked is my sister, my bride. A rock garden locked, a spring sealed up" (Song of Sol. 4:12, NAS).

Just as God alone can dig this well, only He can unlock the garden of our hearts. That's what happened to me one day as I sat in my rocking chair. Something was unlocked. When it became unlocked, I received revelation knowledge from His Word and a fresh understanding of His desire for me. This is the washing of the water of the Word. (See Ephesians 5:26.)

Many different things get in the way and lock up this garden of our hearts. Only the Lord Jesus, the Lover of our souls, can come and unlock the garden within us! He is the One who holds the key, but we must give Him permission to enter and unlock the passageways inside.

Some have said that the key is on the inside, and we are responsible for opening the door. However, He has the combination. He knows the formula that will take that last turn. He knows what will unlock the door and release His presence within us. He does it all.

We may try to make God come to us in the same way He has in the past. But we soon discover that we cannot. I've tried, and it doesn't work. We can never expect that the same types of holy visitations will be repeated in our lives when and how we want them. We just have to wait for Him. God ordains when He will visit, and each encounter is unique and orchestrated by Him.

Chapter 29

A VISION OF ETERNITY
IN HIS PRESENCE

He has also set eternity in the hearts of men.

—Ecclesiastes 3:11, NIV

He was coming—my Beloved, my Friend.* My breath was knocked out of me, and my knees went slack as He came closer. Then, like a tree overtaken by a dust cloud from a wind flurry, the cloud of His glory engulfed me. The spirits still were darting in and lifting out on the periphery, but I could see only Him.

I had seen Him standing in the sanctuary of a church several times before over a period of years.

Now He was standing before me in Paradise.

How can I describe "the Desire of All Nations"? Far more than the impact of His physical appearance, He embodies life. His eyes are clear blue as deep as a bottomless pool. It seems that if you could travel into those eyes, you would understand all mysteries, that in plunging

---

* Anna Rountree, *Heaven Awaits the Bride* (Lake Mary, FL: Charisma House, 2007), 36–46.

toward the bottom of that deep pool, you would pass the answers to all thing.

He embodies love, light, and truth. A kaleidoscope of understanding flooded my spirit, computing faster than lightning, causing me to react as Job reacted when the Lord confronted him—I could only cover my mouth.

He stepped up to me.

He was smiling broadly, as a childhood sweetheart that you knew you would always, always love, but that you had not seen since childhood. The years dropped away as you saw Him, and you were right—you would always, always love Him; no one could ever take His place.

He took my right hand in his left, which strengthened me.

"Come," He said. Immediately we were flying.

Once we landed on the mountains of spices, and without turning His head to look at me, He asked, "Do you wish to bring joy?"

"Yes," I answered.

Jesus responded, "Obedience brings joy to My Father, holiness of heart, thankfulness, truth with mercy. Each is like a spice. Each has a fragrance. Collectively the aromas are pleasing to My Father. The aromas speak of Me to Him, not just one spice but the aroma of the blend as one passes from mountain to mountain. Together they witness of Me, and this pleases My Father. Also the aroma coming from His adopted children speaks of Me, and He is pleased."

I opened my eyes and my right hand to look at a smooth, white stone with the name *Anna* engraved upon it.

"Your new name," He said. "I am adding the breath of life to your name. Here you will be called Anna."

"Anna," I said to myself.

"Now, Anna, My sister and My love, our names have been joined in covenant."

"Thank You," I said, holding the stone to my heart.

"I have been waiting for you, Anna. The loneliness you experienced is nothing compared to the heartache I experienced as I waited for you, seeing you run after all manner of idols to seek satisfaction." He looked out into the garden. "How I called to you." There was pain in His voice. "Year after year you dallied, and I grieved, waiting for you to realize that no one can, or ever will, bring you life itself but Me alone."

His words struck me to the heart. "My Lord and my God," I said quietly, "no one has ever loved me as you have..." I was choked with emotion. Slowly I continued, "Nor has anyone ever desired me my company as...," but I could not finish.

"None of flesh and blood can, Anna, for you belong to Me." He looked me in the eye, and His eyes pierced through me. "I created you for Myself, and only I can satisfy you truly and fully."

I didn't know what to say. I searched, trying to think of some reply. Finally I asked, "If I am created for You, Lord, what can I do for You? How..." I groped for the words to convey that I wanted to give a gift to Him. "How do I give something to You?"

He searched my face for a moment and then smiled. "Sing for Me, Anna; that would comfort Me." He leaned back against the large apricot tree and closed His eyes.

I did not know what to sing. I swallowed hard. Then I looked out over the garden and prayed within myself. Soon, without knowing what I would say, I began to sing.

Chapter 30

A WORD OF HOPE

*And suddenly **there came a sound from heaven,
as of a rushing mighty wind, and it filled the
whole house where they were sitting.***

—ACTS 2:2, NKJV, EMPHASIS ADDED

T HE DEVIL WANTS you to feel hopeless in your situation. He tells you, "Things are never going to be different. You're never going to change. You'll never get your act together, so you might as well give up."*

Well, I have one thing to say about that: the devil is a liar!

You need to know the Word so you can know what God says. And anything that comes to your mind that's opposite of what God's Word says is because God's not saying it! If God's not saying it, and because the devil is a liar, it must not be true.

Regardless of the cause of your disappointment, discouragement, hopelessness, or even depression, there is a word that can give you hope and the courage to reverse the

---

* Mike Purkey, *Reversing the Devil's Decision* (Lake Mary, FL: Charisma House, 2000), 179, 186–188.

devil's decision for your life. I hope you never forget this word: SUDDENLY!

Disappointments, troubles, and circumstances can and do drastically change suddenly! I want to wake up every day with the expectancy that there is no telling what God may suddenly do today!

> When the Day of Pentecost had fully come, they were all with one accord in one place. *And suddenly* there came a sound from heaven, as of a rushing mighty wind, and it filled the whole house where they were sitting.
>
> —ACTS 2:1–2, NKJV,
> EMPHASIS ADDED

The people in the Upper Room had no idea when God would show up or what would happen when He did. But He showed up and poured out His Holy Spirit just as He promised.

And that's the way God wants to move in our lives.

When you've waited and waited and your circumstances still haven't changed. When you feel that you can't stand it one more second, but you're still holding on, trusting God with simple faith.

Then *suddenly* God moves in your life. He often moves when you least expect it. God never appears the way you think. You might be looking out the front door, and He comes in the back door.

That's why we need to stop trying to figure out what God is going to do. One of the greatest burdens you can take on is the burden of trying to figure God out. *"How* is God going to do it? *When* is He going to do it? When, God, when?"

Jesus answered that question in Acts 1:6–7: "Therefore, when they had come together, they asked Him, saying, 'Lord, will You at this time restore the kingdom to Israel?' And He said to them, 'It is not for you to know times or seasons which the Father has put in His own authority'" (NKJV).

The disciples wanted to know when Jesus was going to return, and He answered them, "It is not for you to know the times or seasons." Our responsibility is to wait on God. The responsibility for the timing of His visitation belongs to Him.

There's a Suddenly in Your Life Too

In Acts 16 Paul and Silas were sitting in a jail cell at midnight. Their hands and feet were in stocks. They had been beaten with rods, and now they were bloody and grimy. But they were singing songs, and the other prisoners were listening to them.

Suddenly there was an earthquake. The shackles fell off the prisoners' arms and legs, the prison doors swung wide open, and the captives were set free!

God broke into the middle of their horrible circumstances because circumstances cannot stand for one second before the power of God. That's how great our God is!

But you can't defeat your circumstances without God's help. If you start messing with your circumstances, they may only get worse. In fact, I think we exalt our circumstances to a place that's far too high by paying too much attention to them.

Discouragement sets in when we do everything we know to do and it still doesn't work. That's why we're better off letting God worry about circumstances.

If you or somebody you know is struggling with discouragement, hopelessness, or depression, know this: All at once *suddenly* everything can change. Your job situation can turn around. Your son or daughter can get saved. Any decision the devil has made for your life or the life of your loved one can be reversed.

Rather than frustrating yourself further by trying to change your circumstances, the best thing you can do is wait on God. Spend time in God's presence. Humble yourself before Him and acknowledge to Him that He is the only one who can change your situation. The Bible says, "Therefore humble yourselves under the mighty hand of God, that He may exalt you in due time, casting all your care upon Him, for He cares for you" (1 Pet. 5:6–7, NKJV).

When we get out of God's way, we give Him room to do great things and reverse the devil's decision for discouragement and hopelessness in our lives.

PART 7

HOPE IN
THE WORD OF GOD

Chapter 31

THE KING'S DECREE KEEPS YOUR LIFE ON COURSE

Let them praise the name of the LORD, for He commanded
and they were created. He also established them forever
and ever; He made a decree which shall not pass away.

—PSALM 148:5–6, NKJV

ONE OF THE biggest challenges for every Christian is
forgetting what God said to them. It is the reason
people backslide, give up on their miracles, stop tithing, get
divorced, quit going to church, or even quit serving God
altogether. They get off course when they are put under
pressure. During a trial or moment of frustration, they
forget what they read in the Bible, or after a disappointment they no longer bring to mind the prophetic word they
received.*

It seems as though, when we get tampered with, one of
the first things to go out the window is the Word of the
Lord. Because of this tendency, we have to know how to

---

* Brenda Kunneman, *When Your Life Has Been Tampered With* (Lake
Mary, FL: Charisma House, 2008), 187–191.

hold on to the things we have heard God say so our purpose for Him stays right on target.

In the Book of Ezra, while God's people were busy and excitedly rebuilding the temple under some of the most hellacious attacks, they did something very specific that kept them on course with the project. In Ezra 5 their adversaries had questioned whether they had the right or authority to do the work. The elders overseeing the work answered their adversaries with a powerful comeback: "In the first year of Cyrus the king of Babylon the same king Cyrus *made a decree to build this house of God*" (Ezra 5:13, KJV, emphasis added).

What did the king make? He made a decree. That means he *said* something that he, as the supreme authority, expected to be honored and carried out. There were adversaries, however, who questioned what he had said. They questioned the king's decree.

Notice what the elders did after the word of the king was called into question. They didn't fall apart because this was the last straw. Realize they had been under repeated attacks. The work had been resisted, frustrated, and halted even to the point where it couldn't get going again during the reign of the very king who first told them to do it. You see, so many of us give up when the heat is on at that level. Yet they did one thing. They would not relent with what King Cyrus had decreed. Under tremendous pressure to change what they knew to be true, they went to the current king, Darius, and said, "…let there be search made in the king's treasure house, which is there at Babylon, whether it be so, that a decree was made of Cyrus the king to build this house of God…" (v. 17, KJV).

What did they do? They went back and researched what King Cyrus actually said. Pressure and negative circumstances, combined with people's opinions and disagreements, can cause you to become cloudy with the thing God told you. Trials can make you forget the truth of the Scriptures. Then the temptation is to change direction or change what you believe because you can't handle the resistance. In this case, the elders of Israel were able to hold on to the decree that came from the king because they went back and searched out what was said. They couldn't just try to *remember*; they had to go back and search it out, even though they knew the general idea of the king's decree.

How often do we know the general idea of a prophetic word we received or a biblical truth we once studied? Perhaps you spent the week reading Bible verses on overcoming fear, but after a period of time, when a fearful situation really intimidated you, you forgot to apply what you read. We can all remember times when this has happened.

So the builders of the temple did a review of the king's decree, but did you happen to notice where they went in order to do that review? They went to the king's treasure house. This was the designated place where all the king's laws, decrees, and commandments were archived. For us, King Jesus has designated treasure houses in the spirit where we can go and review what He has decreed over our lives. The first and most obvious treasure house of the King's decrees is the Bible.

You have probably heard the statement: *if you want to know the will of God, read the Word of God.* Depending on what you are standing for in your life, you will need to make a regular search and review of Scripture. Often you will be reviewing the same scriptures again and again. Never think you have gone over the same verses too many times. You have to keep reviewing the Lord's decree for your situation from His treasure house of Scripture. It is just too risky and easy to change Bible truth to fit our circumstances, especially during a trial. Go to the King's treasure house and repeatedly review His written Word so you know what you believe even under pressure and persecution.

Lastly, remember the King's treasure house contains a wealth of His powerful decrees. Those decrees are also found spoken, repeated, and prayed *at church*. By just attending a strong and anointed local church, you will find the King's decree for your life manifesting all around you. Regular contact and fellowship with on-fire believers will open to you a treasure in the spirit. Good, biblical instruction will keep you heading toward the things the Lord is saying instead of allowing you to be sidetracked by whatever might be going on with you personally or with your family.

Chapter 32

GUARDED BY HIS WORD

*Truly, truly, I say to you, if anyone keeps
My word he will never see death.*

—JOHN 8:51, NAS

THE PRIMARY MEANS through which we are kept and preserved by God is through obedience to His Word. In the submission of our will to God, our souls find protection from evil. Consider the apostle John's words to the young men of the first-century church when he said, "I have written to you, young men, because you are strong, and the word of God abides in you, and you have overcome the evil one" (1 John 2:14, NAS).*

Abiding in the Word of God brought spiritual strength to the young men in John's day, enabling them to overcome the evil one. Is this the reason many of us are defeated by the devil—because we do not abide in the Word?

Christ's teaching guides us into the presence of the Father. It is the Father's presence that both empowers and protects us. Jesus said:

---

* Francis Frangipane, *The Shelter of the Most High* (Lake Mary, FL: Charisma House, 2008), 51–56.

> My sheep hear My voice, and I know them, and they follow Me; and I give eternal life to them, and they will never perish; and no one will snatch them out of My hand. My Father, who has given them to Me, is greater than all; and no one is able to snatch them out of the Father's hand.
>
> —JOHN 10:27–29, NAS

No one is stronger than our heavenly Father. As we follow Christ, He positions us in the palm of God's hand. There, death cannot seize us. Whatever battles we face, we never face them alone. There is none like our God. "The eternal God is a dwelling place, and underneath are the everlasting arms; and He drove out the enemy from before you, and said, 'Destroy!'" (Deut. 33:27, NAS).

Underneath our every step are God's everlasting arms. Thus when we pass through spiritual conflicts and trials, we are walking on eternal ground, continually kept by the power of Christ's indestructible life (Heb. 7:16). Even when we pass through the shadow of death itself, the powers of death cannot hold us. They are kept at bay by His command.

> For I am convinced that neither death, nor life, nor angels, nor principalities, nor things present, nor things to come, nor powers, nor height, nor depth, nor any other created thing, shall be able to separate us from the love of God, which is in Christ Jesus our Lord.
>
> —ROMANS 8:38–39, NAS

Those Who Never See Death

The Spirit of God is forever redeeming and transforming all that we encounter, causing each event to work for our spiritual good. Indeed, it has been truly stated that rescue is the constant pattern of God's activity. His final act of encouragement is the Resurrection.

Jesus promised, "Truly, truly, I say to you, if anyone keeps My word he will never see death" (John 8:51, NAS). The Jews to whom Jesus spoke were offended by this statement. They lacked divine logic and the view of life from eternity. They were ignorant of the resurrection power given every follower of Christ.

Before we judge them too harshly, however, let us ask ourselves, "Are we offended by Christ's promise?" Given the fact that everyone who followed Jesus in the first century died, are we ashamed of the apparent contradictions of this promise? Do we really believe we will never see death?

The Jews also were perplexed. They countered, saying, "Now we know that You have a demon. Abraham died, and the prophets also; and You say, 'If anyone keeps My word, he shall never taste of death'" (John 8:52, NAS). But Jesus did not say that His followers would never taste death. He said we would never see death.

Certainly there are times when we seem engulfed by sorrow, trapped in an incubator of death itself. Yet this is a glory of our faith: though we die, we do not see death; we see life. We will taste death, but, as Christians, we ingest life.

Yes, if we keep Christ's Word throughout the trial, His promise to us is that we will "never see death." For those who live by every word that comes from the mouth of God, the final outcome of each struggle is not death but life in abundance.

As we keep Christ's Word, our difficulties always culminate in eternal life. We join Paul in thanking God, "Who always leads us in triumph in Christ, and manifests through us the sweet aroma of the knowledge of Him in every place" (2 Cor. 2:14, NAS).

There will be a time when, from the vantage point of heaven, we will review our life's experiences. In glorious retrospect we shall see every occasion when destruction stood against us. And we will also see that it was here, in these very difficulties, that Christ revealed within us His resurrection power! Though we walked through the valley of the shadow of death, we did not die. Rather, we learned to fear no evil. From heaven's view, with awe we will one day say, "Truly, I have never seen death."

Chapter 33

WORDS WORTH AGREEING WITH

All the promises of God in Him are Yes, and in
Him Amen, to the glory of God through us.
—2 CORINTHIANS 1:20, NKJV

WHEN YOU READ one of God's promises to you in
the Bible, what is you first thought? Do you think,
"Oh, it will be wonderful to have that someday in heaven,"
or "What a wonderful promise! Of course, that is not for
somebody as miserable as me." Or do you think, "Praise
God! If He says that I should have that, then nothing can
stop His blessing from manifesting in my life!"*

Unfortunately too many pick the first two. Just as the
Israelites did standing on the Jordan looking at what was
promised to them, we too often choose to give up before
the battle even begins.

Did you know that some of the greatest Christians of
all times were lawyers? Now, we tend to make fun of lawyers and politicians in our culture today, but throughout
history lawyers have revealed some of the greatest things

---

* Cindy Trimm, *Commanding Your Morning* (Lake Mary, FL: Charisma
House, 2007), 59–62.

about God we have ever known. Moses was "the lawgiver," and the apostle Paul was a Pharisee. (The Pharisees were a group who studied the Word of God as the law book on which to govern society.) Martin Luther of the Reformation began his career by entering law school, as did the great revivalist Charles Finney. What made them so powerful? They read their Bibles as lawyers would when studying to prepare a case, and they put more faith in God keeping His Word than they did in any earthly laws or political promises. Then they took those words and charged the atmosphere around them with biblical truth. They changed their worlds through what they spoke.

Look at what happened when Ezekiel took God at His Word and spoke it into a dead atmosphere: "So I prophesied as I was commanded; and as I prophesied, there was a noise, and suddenly a rattling; and the bones came together, bone to bone. Indeed, as I looked, the sinews and the flesh came upon them, and the skin covered them over; but there was no breath in them. Then He said to me, 'Prophesy to the breath, prophesy, son of man, and say to the breath, "Thus says the Lord God: 'Come from the four winds, O breath, and breathe on these slain, that they may live.'"' So I prophesied as He commanded me, and breath came in to them, and they lived, and stood on their feet, an exceeding great army" (Ezek. 37:7–10, NKJV).

When you read the Bible, you need to take God's Word personally. His promises are for His people, and if you have given your life to Him as your Lord and Savior, then that means YOU. Speak life into your dead areas—you'll be amazed at what God's words in your mouth will do for you.

Chapter 34

THE SCRIPTURES INSPIRE US WITH DIVINE POWER

The word of God is living and powerful, and sharper than any two-edged sword, piercing even to the division of soul and spirit, and of joints and marrow, and is a discerner of the thoughts and intents of the heart.

—HEBREWS 4:12, NKJV

IF INDEED "NOTHING succeeds like success," then nothing will succeed more than prayer, for behind our praying are the living and powerful promises of the Bible. David sang, "This poor man cried out, and the LORD heard him, and saved him out of all his troubles." And then he implored, "Oh, taste and see that the LORD is good; blessed is the man who trusts in Him!...Those who seek the LORD shall not lack any good thing" (Ps. 34:6, 8, 10, NKJV). David saw prayer as powerful enough to produce results because it dealt with the almighty God who was able to do anything.*

The Holy Spirit is most persuasive in bringing us to prayer,

---

* Judson Cornwall, *Praying the Scriptures* (Lake Mary, FL: Charisma House, 1988, 1997, 2008), 79–80.

and the commands of the Scriptures are completely author-itative. But there is something beyond this that inspires us to earnest praying. God's Word is powerful, because all the power of God's inherent nature stands behind it. God said it, and that settles it! There are no promises greater than God's ability to perform. The Scriptures assure us, "The word of God is living and powerful, and sharper than any two-edged sword, piercing even to the division of soul and spirit, and of joints and marrow, and is a discerner of the thoughts and intents of the heart" (Heb. 4:12, NKJV). It is likely that the first evidence of the power of the Word will be in us. God's Word is living, so when we incorporate the Scriptures into our prayers, God's life works in us. I have seen this happen.

Once I was ministering with my sister and a most com-petent staff to a group of ministers and their wives. The ses-sions extended from eight in the morning until ten at night. The conferees were exhausted by the time the final evening class convened. Just prior to my speaking, a music min-ister was asked to lead some choruses from the piano. He played a few bars of a song to get our attention and then asked us to open our Bibles to Psalm 150 and stand. We all expected to be led in singing this psalm, but, instead, he had us read it in unison. I confess that I was amazed at the results. As we read that psalm with feeling, we seemed to release fresh faith toward God, and divine energy flowed out of each of us. The power of God's Word overcame the physical exhaustion we had brought in to the room, and it inspired us to worship the Lord. The singing that followed was electric, the response to the teaching was thrilling, and the season of prayer we had after the teaching was powerful.

We had been made alive by the simple act of reading aloud a portion of Scripture during our devotional time.

The Old Testament declares it, and the New Testament affirms that "man shall not live by bread alone; but man lives by every word that proceeds from the mouth of the LORD" (Deut. 8:3, NKJV; see also Luke 4:4). There is physical strength and energy available in God when we use the Scriptures in our praying. What an inspiration this should be to "pray continually" (1 Thess. 5:17, NIV).

Praying the Scriptures not only inspires our prayers, but it also illuminates those prayers. When the psalmist stated, "The unfolding of your words gives light; it gives understanding to the simple" (Ps. 119:130, NIV), he understood that the Scriptures illuminate our every contact with God.

Chapter 35

CONFESS HOPE

Hold fast the confession of our hope without
wavering, for He who promised is faithful.
—Hebrews 10:23, NAS

FOR A MOMENT, forget that you are reading, and
imagine that you and I are sitting face-to-face in your
favorite getaway. Look me in the eye. I'm asking you to
make a permanent commitment to a lifestyle of hope, no
matter what, even if at first you see no apparent change in
your situation. *Are you willing to choose the paradigm of hope*
right now, to start saying about yourself what God says about
you? I will assume your answer is yes.*

Look at the Declarations of Hope below, and repeat
them aloud, beginning each with either "I will stop
saying" or "I will start saying." Talking aloud might
seem a bit strange, since you are probably either reading
alone or next to a sleeping spouse. But as we shall see
later, saying them with your mouth is important. Now,
go ahead and make your declarations.

---

* Terry Law and Jim Gilbert, *The Hope Habit* (Lake Mary, FL: Charisma
House, 2010), 202–204, 209–210.

DECLARATIONS OF HOPE	
I will stop saying:	**I will start saying:**
My situation is hopeless.	I am confident in the goodness of God. There is hope for me.
I hate waking up in the morning.	The Lord's mercies are new every morning, and His faithfulness is great. Therefore I will hope in him (Lam. 3:22–24).
My bills are overwhelming; I'm even afraid to answer the phone.	My God will supply all my needs according to His riches in glory in Christ Jesus (Phil. 4:19).
I don't deserve another chance.	I will draw near with confidence to God's throne, where I can receive mercy and find grace to help in my time of need (Heb. 4:16).
Nothing ever works out for me.	I believe God has plans for me, for good and not for evil, to give me a future and a hope (Jer. 29:11).
My father did this to me.	I am a new creation in Christ Jesus. My past has been wiped out; everything has become new (2 Cor. 5:17).
My country is too far gone; I can't make a difference.	I will humble myself and pray and seek God's face, turning away from wickedness, so that God will hear from heaven, forgive our sins, and heal our land (2 Chron. 7:14).
My problems are too big to solve.	Nothing is impossible with God (Luke 1:37).

DECLARATIONS OF HOPE	
I will stop saying:	**I will start saying:**
God has forgotten me. I feel so alone in the world.	I am the apple of God's eye; He hides me in the shadow of His wings (Ps. 17:8).
I'm damaged goods. Who would ever want to marry me?	Therefore there is now no condemnation for me, because I am in Christ Jesus (Rom. 8:1).
I can't raise these children by myself.	I can do all things through Him who strengthens me (Phil. 4:13).
My professor makes a fool of me.	Men will see my good works and glorify my Father who is in heaven (Matt. 5:16).
I'll never break free of this habit.	Yet in all these things we are more than conquerors through Him who loved us (Rom. 8:37).
I'll never get well.	By His stripes I was healed (1 Pet. 2:24).
It's not my fault. I'm the victim here. I've been cheated, abused, ripped off.	I have worked harder, been put in jail more often, been whipped times without number, and faced death again and again....If I must boast, I would rather boast about the things that show how weak I am (2 Cor. 11:23, 30).

Every positive statement you just made about yourself was a personalized version of one or more verses of the Holy Scriptures. Why use passages from the Bible as an antidote to hopelessness? *Because the cure for what you say about your situation is what God says about your situation!*

Your Confession of Hope

What you have done here by speaking aloud the above declarations is called a *confession* of hope in the Bible. I use the term *declaration* for clarity's sake since most people associate the word *confession* with an admission of wrongdoing. But *confess* is actually more precise, because the word means "to speak the same." When you confess the truth, you are merely aligning your words with the facts of the matter. With this in mind, look at Hebrews 10:23, which encourages us to "hold fast the confession of our hope without wavering, for He who promised is faithful" (NAS).

The imagery in that sentence is almost nautical. When life comes at you like a storm, the hope-filled words of your mouth will steer you through, as though your tongue were a rudder to keep you on course. Actually, this very metaphor was used by the apostle James, who called the tongue a "very small rudder" that steers the whole person (James 3:4–6, NAS).

But how does holding fast to your confession of hope keep you from crashing? Is it mind over matter? Not at all. The rest of Hebrews 10:23 explains why you must hold fast without wavering: "For He who promised is faithful" (NAS). *God is faithful to fulfill the promises that you continue confessing in hope.*

PART 8

HOPE EVERLASTING

Chapter 36

DON'T JUST HANG IN THERE—STAND!

*Therefore take up the whole armor of God, that
you may be able to withstand in the evil day, and
having done all, to stand. Stand, therefore . . .*
—EPHESIANS 6:13–14, NKJV

SOME OF THE most valuable life lessons I have learned
were taught by my mother. In terms of faith, endurance, and resilience, my mother is the most solid woman I
know—one who maintains great dignity and exudes quiet
strength. I have watched her stand strong in the face of
adversity . . . especially since my father's passing.*

During recent years without Dad, my mother has stayed
the course, trusting God always, even at those times when
there seemed to be no answers. Her secret is simple. Once,
addressing an audience of women, she said people often
tried to comfort her by encouraging her to "hang in there."

Never at a loss for words, Mom shared her own unique

---

* Babbie Mason, *Treasures of Heaven in the Stuff of Earth* (Lake Mary,
FL: Charisma House, 2000), 38–41.

interpretation of that phrase—and her words encouraged me more than most sermons I've heard!

"You could hang in there," my mother said, "but you don't *want* to hang in there. When you're *hanging*, you're out of control, dangling by a thread, holding on for dear life. You are vulnerable to your circumstances.

"To hang in there is to be like a sheet on your grand-mother's clothesline, exposed to rain, dust, and other elements that can sneak up behind and take it by surprise. The neighbor's children could run through the yard, snatching the sheet to the ground and leaving it ruined.

"It's not good to be in a hanging position. The only picture I can conjure up is that of a noose. So you don't ever want to hang! It means you have no course of action, just a neutral position, relinquishing all control. When you're in spiritual warfare, this mind-set can mean certain death!

"Instead, as Ephesians 6:13–14 says, 'Therefore take up the whole armor of God, that you may be able to withstand in the evil day, and having done all, to stand. Stand, there-fore...' [NKJV].

"So," my mother concluded, "you don't ever want to just hang in there. Jesus Christ was hung up for our hang-ups so we could stand up, firm and strong, on the promises in His Word!"

My mother's advice—"Don't just hang in there, but STAND"—has carried me through tough times. I hope her words offer you strength to forge through tough times of your own. The forces of the enemy are very real, but God has provided us with every weapon needed to make us more than conquerors.

From head to toe, He has equipped us for battle. He

gave us the belt of truth so we can remain established in the face of error and never waver. He dressed us with the breastplate of righteousness so we can stand against lawlessness and injustice. He placed our feet on a sure foundation, enabling us to carry the good news of the gospel into a dark and chaotic world. The shield of faith protects us from the flaming arrows of the enemy. The helmet of salvation is ours as we experience God's sure deliverance. God has armed us with the sword of the Spirit, which is the Word of God, empowering us to keep our enemies at bay.

Notice, however, that God's armor covers only the front. He does not intend for us to cower and run, allowing the enemy to take potshots at our rear.

So take it from the apostle Paul—and my mother. After you've done all you know to do, don't hang in there. Keep standing. After you have prayed all you know how to pray and cried until there are no more tears, STAND FIRM.

When there is too much month and too little money, STAND. If people promised they'd be there when the going got tough, but left you alone and holding the bag, establish yourself. When the only certainty in your life is uncertainty and the bottom is dropping out from beneath you, keep standing.

Then, God's people discover that when you get to the bottom, you will find the bottom is firm and secure, and you will still be able to stand on the principles and promises of God's Word.

Chapter 37

SIGNPOSTS TO THE
PROMISED LAND

Your ears shall hear a word behind you,
saying, "This is the way, walk in it."
—ISAIAH 30:21, NKJV

JESUS WALKED STRAIGHT through the wilderness by
following the signposts found in Scripture. The children of Israel made a career of their wilderness experience by refusing to obey the Lord's direction. Even after
they walked out of the land of their captivity, their hearts
remained full of idolatrous habits and negative attitudes,
formed by four hundred years of slavery. They were out of
Egypt, but Egypt was still in them.*

Let me ask you a question: Have you truly left Egypt?
Are you looking back at a past relationship, a lost promotion, a bitter experience? Is your mind so fixed on a person
or a situation that it keeps you from going forward with
your life? What was once hard to bear is often sweet to

---

* John Hagee, *Life's Challenges, Your Opportunities* (Lake Mary, FL: Charisma House, 2010), 137–138, 141–143, 145, 158–162, 164–168, 170.

remember. "Do not say, 'Why were the former days better than these?' For you do not inquire wisely concerning this" (Eccles. 7:10, NKJV).

Quit looking back at "what might have been" and refusing to enter into God's gracious provision of "what can be," because God will leave you "in" your problem until you follow the signposts found in His Word that lead you "out" of the problem.

Signpost #1—Faith

The first signpost out of the wilderness is faith—not faith that God can do it, but faith that God will do it—for you, and do it right now.

Faith opens the windows of heaven and closes the gates of hell. Faith is the daring of the soul to see farther than the natural eyes can see. The Bible says, "As it is written, 'The just shall live by faith'" (Rom. 1:17, NKJV).

Faith reverses the natural order. In the natural, we see and then we believe. Hence, we say, "Seeing is believing." By faith we first believe it, and then we see it in the natural. That's why the Bible says, "We walk by faith and not by sight."

Mark 9:23 says, "Jesus said to him, 'If you can believe, all things are possible to him who believes'" (NKJV). The sequence is this: you believe first and receive later. The carnal man wants to receive it first and then believes he has it after it's in his hand.

Faith has "substance." Faith is real. It is measurable. Substance in this case means that we have an assurance that God will do for us today what He has done for His people previously. God's past performance gives us absolute assurance for our future.

The Bible says, "Have faith in God." Faith in God is more than crossing your fingers and saying, "I hope, I hope, I hope." Faith in God is substance based on the Word of God and the evidence of God's past performance. Not only is the object of your faith important, but so is its source.

Signpost #2—Diligence

The Christian life is intended to be a life of diligence. Diligence is characterized by steady, earnest, and energetic effort. Diligence is like an intense laser beam focused on a specific goal.

Diligence is Saint Paul saying, "This one thing I do." Paul didn't dabble in a dozen different areas and preach the gospel on the side. With laser-beam intensity he focused on the "prize of the high calling of God in Christ Jesus" (Phil. 3:14, KJV).

How diligent are you in your service to Christ? How diligent are you in your covenant with your spouse? How diligent are you in the provision and protection of your family? Diligence is not an option; it is a command of God. Diligence is a vital signpost out of your problem. Proverbs 4:23 says, "Keep thy heart with all diligence; for out of it are the issues of life" (KJV).

Signpost #3—Excellence

Everyone possesses the potential for greatness. You are the divine creation of a majestic God, who is committed to excellence. There is within you His divine spark of excellence, waiting to explode into its blazing and brilliant potential.

You are God's divine creation, and locked within you is the spirit of excellence. You are designed for high flight. It's God's will for you to achieve excellence, even while you are in the middle of the problem. Psalm 16:3 states, "As for the saints who are on the earth, 'They are the excellent ones, in whom is all my delight'" (NKJV).

God's divine assignment for you is a land flowing with milk and honey. You have a special purpose on this earth that only you can accomplish. You must choose to accomplish it with excellence for the glory of God and the realization of your dream.

Excellence is not a project, act, or job description; excellence is a way of life. It includes going beyond the normal call of duty, stretching our perceived limits, and holding ourselves responsible for being our best.

Excellence is simply doing your very best, in everything, in every way, in every situation.

Signpost #4—Knowledge

> But also for this very reason, giving all diligence,
> add to your faith virtue, to virtue knowledge.
> —2 PETER 1:5, NKJV

The word for knowledge in 2 Peter is the Greek word *gnosis*, meaning "to know God and his salvation."[1] "Grace and peace be multiplied to you in the knowledge of God and of Jesus our Lord" (v. 2, NKJV).

In verse 2 the word *knowledge* is the Greek word *epignosis*, meaning, "super knowledge."[2] Saint Paul, writing to the Colossian believers, prayed that they might have the *epignosis*, meaning the super knowledge of God (Col. 1:9). The Gnostic heresy, which covered the earth in that day, claimed to impart super knowledge through the secret rituals.

However, for both Peter and Paul, knowledge meant growth and development in the Christian life, and super knowledge was their goal as the Holy Spirit confirmed the Word of God to the individual believer.

God can give you the word of knowledge if you will seek His face in the day of your problem. The word of knowledge is a supernatural revelation of information pertaining to a person or an event, given for a specific purpose, usually having to do with an immediate need.[3] The God whom we serve is the God who reveals secret things to His children. This is promised in Deuteronomy 29:29: "The secret things belong to the LORD our God, but the things revealed belong to us and to our children forever" (NIV).

Your denomination may not believe in the word of knowledge, but I assure you on the authority of God's Word and the teaching of Saint Paul, it's very real and very available if you're willing to seek the face of God to know the unknowable and to do the impossible. It is God's laser beam that will guide you straight through the problem.

Signpost #5—Patience

If God left His precious, perfect, and only begotten Son in the problem for forty days, why do you believe that God has failed you if in the next forty minutes He doesn't solve the problem you've embraced for the past forty years? Like the children of Israel, we ignore God when we are problem free but demand that He take us out of our troubles just minutes after we come into them.

Most people have the wrong concept of the word *patience*. Patience is, in fact, the ability to endure when trials come while you're in the problem. Patience is, in other words, endurance.

Saint Paul wrote that we are to "endure hardness, as a good soldier of Jesus Christ" (2 Tim. 2:3, KJV). According to the apostle, God expects you to demonstrate endurance.

Endurance is divine. The Bible says in Matthew 24:13, "He who endures to the end shall be saved" (NKJV). In James 5:11 we see the result of endurance: "Behold, we count them happy which endure" (KJV).

Endurance is the road less traveled, but it is the road to all accomplishment. Endurance is a choice you make every day of your life. James 1:3–4 says, "Knowing this, that the trying of your faith worketh patience. But let patience have her perfect work, that ye may be perfect and entire, wanting nothing" (KJV). We must learn to endure the winds of adversity for they lead us to the highest pinnacle of success.

Endurance will carry you through the problem you are in to the provision you must have! It's always too soon to quit!

Signpost #6—Integrity

Integrity has become a rare and precious commodity in America. *Integrity* is defined in Webster's Dictionary as "adherence to a code of moral or other values."

The Bible demands integrity for all successful leaders. Proverbs 11:3 says, "The integrity of the upright shall guide them: but the perverseness of transgressors shall destroy them" (KJV).

You pass or fail in life based on your personal integrity! Without integrity you will never reach the promised land.

Without integrity you will never walk out of your problem and into God's provision for your life.

Chapter 38

DON'T RING THE BELL!

...they should always pray and not give up.
—Luke 18:1, niv

THE FIRST PHASE of training to be a Navy SEAL lasts a grueling eight weeks. Midway through this rigorous basic conditioning session comes *Hell Week*. The intensity ratchets up significantly during this ultimate test of mental, physical, and emotional strength. Candidates only get 4 hours of sleep during the 132-hour period. And they are wet and cold the entire time. They are required to swim through mud, push logs up sand hills, and carry boats with their bare hands, all while dealing with chafing, bleeding, open sores, and tired muscles.*

To compound the sheer fatigue, trainees are yelled at—in fact, taunted—throughout the process. With expletive-laced tirades they are offered incentives to quit. And more than 70 percent do just that. A large bell hangs prominently at this Special Warfare Center. And regardless of who rings it and whatever time it's rung, the sound signals that

---

* David D. Ireland, *The Kneeling Warrior* (Lake Mary, FL: Charisma House, 2013), 39–56.

a SEAL trainee has quit. For that individual the almost insane training is over. His helmet is removed and placed on the ground beneath the bell. He has declared publicly that becoming a Navy SEAL simply isn't worth it. He's chosen to remain an ordinary soldier rather than to endure the rigor, discipline, and mental anguish needed to join the elite ranks of the Navy SEALs.

Don't Quit!

In Luke 18:1 Jesus taught His twelve recruits "that they should always pray and not give up" (NIV). Jesus's message is: "Don't quit! Don't ring the bell!" His counsel is followed by a parable of a persistent widow who illustrates the value of a prayer-filled lifestyle.

This widow sought justice through the local judge. Because the judge was corrupt, he refused to grant her justice though she appeared before him several times. The judge's disregard for victims like this widow was further compromised by his irreverence of the Lord. But the widow was unmoved by the judge's lack of compassion and his penchant for bribes. Her persistence resulted in a favorable ruling. The judge grew sick and tired of her repeated requests for justice (vv. 4–6). It was purely her unmitigated persistence that had worn him down.

The parable of the persistent widow reinforces our call to vigilance and persistence in prayer. Although she didn't receive her answer the first time she asked, the widow ultimately gained the justice she sought through her persistence. And she symbolizes Jesus's message to us, "Don't quit! Don't ring the bell!", even in the face of delay and hardship.

The parable ends with this statement: "And will not God bring about justice for his chosen ones, who cry out to him day and night? Will he keep putting them off? I tell you, he will see that they get justice, and quickly" (vv. 7–8, NIV). God expects us to cry out to Him day and night. Unlike the unjust judge, God won't ignore our pleas for justice.

The Bible clearly states, "The prayer of the upright pleases him" (Prov. 15:8, NIV). God's power matches the generosity of His heart. It is a fundamental teaching of the Bible that God is omnipotent—all powerful. So don't give in to discouragement and prayerlessness when the fire of life's trials intensify; God hears you and wants to answer your prayers.

The widow woman knew that her persistence meant she'd have to "ask." And she repeatedly asked the judge for justice. Jesus underscored this when He said, "They should always pray and not give up" (Luke 18:1, NIV). With this thought in mind Martin Luther said, "When I get hold of a promise…I look upon as I would a fruit tree….If I would get them I must shake the tree to and fro."[1]

God wants us to make requests because He delights in answering us. We ought to persistently pursue Him for all His promises because this pleases Him.

And while God loves us and wants our best, He cannot ignore His own laws of prayer. There are four common reasons for unanswered prayers:

1. The prayer may reflect wrong motives and dishonest motivations (James 4:2–3).

2. The prayer may be outside of God's will (1 John 5:14–15).

3. The prayer is not followed up with action.

4. The person praying may doubt God's ability or willingness to answer the prayer (James 1:6–8).

Don't despair if your prayers are not being answered. Instead, examine your request to determine whether it violates any of the laws of prayer mentioned above. If it does, abandon the request and ask the Holy Spirit for direction in how to pray to see breakthrough in your situation. He is our helper in prayer (Rom. 8:26).

The parable of the persistent widow is a lesson about how we should pray and never give up. She emulates what it means to have faith in God in the face of human opposition and a blatant disregard for justice. We can extract from this parable that the widow was not merely praying mechanical prayers—those bereft of the true sentiment of heart and a genuine embrace of God's will, leaving one deprived of the fruitfulness of a Spirit-directed life. Mechanical prayers are stiff and stilted and don't produce the answers you desire from the Lord. Faith in God, on the other hand, is fluid. It calls for an ongoing emotional and spiritual engagement. You must decide to believe God. You must intentionally choose to trust in God's promises...today.

Don't allow the words of Jesus to fall to the earth without bearing fruit. Pray without giving up. By keeping this command, the joy of obedience will be yours, and the mystery surrounding prayer will be unveiled to you since God delights in answering prayers. This is the command of our General: Don't ring the bell until you hear Jesus's command to lay down your arms and cease praying!

Chapter 39

THE GUMPTION TO GO!

The LORD himself goes before you and will be with you; he will never leave you nor forsake you. Do not be afraid; do not be discouraged.

—DEUTERONOMY 31:8, NIV

G*UMPTION* IS A very interesting word. It could be used to describe someone who has "guts" or nerve or courage. It makes me think of the saying, "Faith is courage that has said its prayers." If you don't miss your moment and you walk on in faith to meet it, you have the "gumption to go."*

Peter was a "gumptor." Peter had a very interesting life after he met Jesus. Whether it was walking on water (Matt. 14), going up the mountain to see Jesus transfigured (Matt. 17; Mark 9; Luke 9), or tangling with the crowd in the Garden of Gethsemane (Matt. 26; Mark 14; Luke 22; John 18), Peter was 100 percent involved. He didn't always do the right thing. He was impulsive by nature, and that got him into trouble more than once. (I'm thinking of Matthew 26:34: "...before the

---

* Judy Jacobs, *Don't Miss Your Moment* (Lake Mary, FL: Charisma House, 2008), 173–178.

rooster crows, you will deny Me three times" [NKJV].) But he always rallied. He always came around. Jesus even made sure that he was restored after he had denied Him, allowing Peter to be one of the first people to see the empty tomb and, in the most touching moment of them all, talking with him one-to-one on the beach and telling him, "Feed My lambs.... Tend My sheep.... Feed My sheep" (John 21:15–17, NKJV).

You could say that Peter's life consisted of an amazing series of God moments. And because so many of them are described in the Bible, we can see how he responded to them. We know about the ones he missed as well as the ones he didn't. Peter's life as a disciple and a follower of Jesus pulls open the curtains to reveal something very special—the incredible way the Lord Himself makes every effort to help Peter—and us—connect with Him.

After Jesus's resurrection Peter followed the Holy Spirit, and he had many more adventures. He had gotten a lot better at listening to the Spirit instead of forging ahead under his own steam. Even so, more than once he might have missed his moment to act if the Lord Himself hadn't sent help. For instance, remember what happened when he was locked up in prison?

> Peter was therefore kept in prison, but constant prayer was offered to God for him by the church. And when Herod was about to bring him out, that night Peter was sleeping, bound with two chains between two soldiers; and the guards before the door were keeping the prison. Now behold, an angel of the Lord stood by him, and a light shone in the prison; and he struck Peter on the side and

raised him up, saying, "Arise quickly!" And his chains fell off his hands. Then the angel said to him, "Gird yourself and tie on your sandals"; and so he did. And he said to him, "Put on your garment and follow me." So he went out and followed him, and did not know that what was done by the angel was real, but thought he was seeing a vision. When they were past the first and the second guard posts, they came to the iron gate that leads to the city, which opened to them of its own accord; and they went out and went down one street, and immediately the angel departed from him.

—Acts 12:5–10, NKJV

That was quite a God moment, and Peter did not miss it. (Neither would I if an angel struck me on my side and ordered me to my feet!) God made sure of it. Because of God's power, Peter had the gumption to go and do something that otherwise would have been very foolish to try, not to mention impossible to achieve. Nobody just gets up and walks out of prison scot-free like that. With God's angel leading him, Peter did.

That is encouraging to me personally. Even strong and forceful Peter might have missed that moment of escape and deliverance if he had been left to his own devices. There really was precious little he could have done in his own strength to get out of that situation. You see, along with an angelic encounter, God sent Peter the courage and obedience and faith and just plain *gumption* that would be required to follow through. Another way to look at it is to say that God most definitely gave Peter what I call the "go ye" that he needed.

(Notice, however, that in the midst of all the supernatural shakings and quakings, Peter had to bend over and put on his own sandals and pull his clothes on by himself. He had to move on his own. The angel didn't clothe him supernaturally and transport him out of the dungeon in a fiery chariot.)

Although he thought it was a dream at first, Peter walked out of there on his own two feet. He didn't worry about the next locked door ahead. He didn't spend any time looking over his shoulder for the guards' pursuit. He just proceeded out with the angel in the lead. And when the angel disappeared, he carried on alone, walking to his friends' house without an escort. Don't you think Peter had to have some extra gumption in order to get up and go like that?

When a moment of God's call comes to you, you may or may not be in some kind of a prison. It may happen to you when you're running a load of clothes in the wash or driving down the street in your car. I don't think you will have very much trouble recognizing God's touch if you have gotten very far in your life. In other words, you probably will not miss your moment.

However, to make your moment count, you need to be like Peter; you need to make sure that you have the "go ye." You need to make sure you have not only your marching orders and a sense of anointing, but also the courage to go forth and do whatever God has called you to do. To make sure your God moment doesn't just blow away in the wind and land somewhere else, you need to exercise the right combination of obedience and anointing.

You need to get up on your own two feet and put on your shoes (of faith), and then you need to follow the leading of the Holy Spirit as obediently as you possibly can, asking for more of God's help every step of the way. As you do so, amazing things will start to happen. The purposes of God will start to be realized in and through your life.

Chapter 40

KEEP MOVING FORWARD

Forget the former things; do not dwell on the
past. See, I am doing a new thing! Now it springs
up; do you not perceive it? I am making a way
in the desert and streams in the wasteland.

—Isaiah 43:18-19, NIV

In *The Anointing: Three Eras* R. T. Kendall shares the story of what inspired his outstanding, prophetic book.* One day while reading 1 Samuel 16:1, a penetrating truth leaped out at him:

> The Lord said to Samuel, "How long will you mourn for Saul, since I have rejected him as king over Israel? Fill your horn with oil and be on your way; I am sending you to Jesse of Bethlehem. I have chosen one of his sons to be king."
>
> —NIV

---

* Larry Tomczak, *Reckless Abandon* (Lake Mary, FL: Charisma House, 2002), 13–14, 19–20.

"In a flash," Kendall comments, "I saw three eras: yesterday's man (King Saul), today's man (Samuel), and tomorrow's man (David)."[1]

For the rest of his book Kendall challenges his readers to keep advancing with God's ongoing purposes, lest they become yesterday's people and miss out on God's purposes today. He quotes Jim Bakker, who admits:

> [I] had become yesterday's man and for years didn't know it, still moving and working in the gifts I had received in the past. God had a new message for me, a new life. God wanted to make me into tomorrow's man. That's not an easy task.[2]

Having walked through this traumatic, midlife directional change, I stand on the other side to encourage you before you come to your proverbial fork in the road. Through my own pilgrimage into the unknown I have learned that even when you are wallowing in utter stagnation and barrenness, when you are drowning in challenging circumstances and vehement criticism, the Holy Spirit can still infuse you with supernatural strength—not strength merely to endure, but strength to enter a fresh move of God. That is, if you walk humbly, circumspectly, and obediently—no matter what the cost.

You will face your *refining* moments—they're inevitable. But you are never guaranteed that they will become your *defining* moments. Many Christians live their entire lives as yesterday's people. They subsist on day-old manna and relish the past rather than anticipate the future. They may not even recognize the meagerness of their existence because it has become all too familiar. But deep inside they hunger for something more.

You may even be at this juncture in your life. But whether you are or not: I ask you: Are you tomorrow's man or woman?

Do you sense in your spirit that God is up to something? Do you ever wonder if God is attempting to use difficult, sometimes even seemingly impossible situations to bring you into a new refreshing season of the Spirit?

The God we serve is a God of newness. His Word speaks of receiving new wine in new wineskins, enjoying a new heart, having a new name, singing a new song, and proclaiming a new and living way. The words of Isaiah 43:18–19 have great significance for today: "Forget the former things; do not dwell on the past. See, I am doing a new thing! Now it springs up; do you not perceive it? I am making a way in the desert and streams in the wasteland" (NIV).

But in order to enter this new season of refreshing, you must be willing to pay the price—death. Death to your agenda. Death to your old habits. Death to a risk-free life. Death to your old selfish ways. Jesus said, "I tell you the truth, unless a kernel of wheat falls to the ground and dies, it remains only a single seed. But if it dies, it produces many seeds" (John 12:24, NIV).

Are you willing to pay the price to come into the fullness of what God ordained for your life in this historic hour?

Fortunately, the fruit of this sacrifice is nothing short of God's purpose and provision. "'For I know the plans I have for you,' says the LORD, 'plans to prosper you and not to harm you, plans to give you hope and a future'" (Jer. 29:11, NIV).

Don't listen to Satan's manipulative lies declaring, "Your best days are behind you. God is finished with you."

Close your ears to the lies from Satan, and begin to listen to the truth from God. The best is yet to come for your life.

NOTES

Chapter 5
God's Amazing Grace Will Cover Your Failures

1. "Amazing Grace" by John Newton. Public domain.
2. Ibid.

Chapter 12
A Winning Strategy for Victory

1. A. B. Simpson, *Thirty-One Kings: Or Victory Over Self* (Harrisburg, PA: Christian Publications, Inc., 1992).
2. Fuchsia Pickett, *Placed in His Glory* (Lake Mary, FL: Charisma House, 2001), 126–127.

Chapter 37
Signposts to the Promised Land

1. J. Vernon McGee, *Thru the Bible*, vol. 5 (Nashville: Thomas Nelson, 1990), 722.
2. Ibid.
3. Jack Hayford, general editor, *The Spirit-Filled Life Bible* (Nashville: Thomas Nelson, 1991), 1736.

Chapter 38
Don't Ring the Bell!

1. As quoted in Charles H. Spurgeon, "A Lecture for Little-Faith," in *Faith in All Its Splendor* (N.p.: Sovereign Grace Publishers, 2006), 11.

Chapter 40
Keep Moving Forward

1. R. T. Kendall, *The Anointing: Three Eras* (London: Hodder and Stoughton, 1999), ix.
2. Ibid., quoting Jim Bakker in the Foreword, xiv.

FREE NEWSLETTERS
TO HELP EMPOWER YOUR LIFE

Why subscribe today?

❑ **DELIVERED DIRECTLY TO YOU.** All you have to do is open your inbox and read.

❑ **EXCLUSIVE CONTENT.** We cover the news overlooked by the mainstream press.

❑ **STAY CURRENT.** Find the latest court rulings, revivals, and cultural trends.

❑ **UPDATE OTHERS.** Easy to forward to friends and family with the click of your mouse.

CHOOSE THE E-NEWSLETTER THAT INTERESTS YOU MOST:

- Christian news
- Daily devotionals
- Spiritual empowerment
- And much, much more

SIGN UP AT: **http://freenewsletters.charismamag.com**

8178